# Grammar Activities

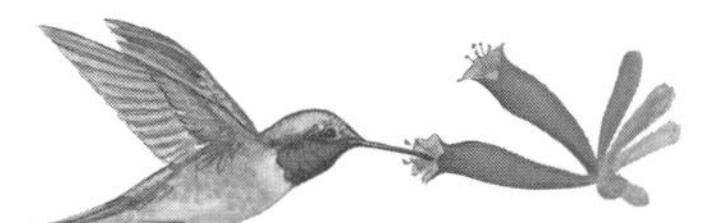

FOR

THE OXFORD

# Picture Dictionary

Jayme Adelson-Goldstein
Norma Shapiro

198 Madison Avenue
New York, NY 10016 USA

Great Clarendon Street
Oxford OX2 6DP England

*Oxford New York*
*Auckland Bangkok Buenos Aires Cape Town Chennai*
*Dar es Salaam Delhi Hong Kong Istanbul Karachi Kolkata*
*Kuala Lumpur Madrid Melbourne Mexico City Mumbai*
*Nairobi São Paulo Shanghai Taipei Tokyo Toronto*



ISBN 0-19-438406-3



Editorial Manager: Janet Aitchison
Editors: Diane Piniaris, Margaret Brooks
Art Director: Lynn Luchetti
Production Manager: Shanta Persaud
Production Controller: Eve Wong

**Authors' acknowledgments**

The authors wish to thank Diane Piniaris, and Meg Brooks for sharing their expertise and sense of humor during the writing process. We would also like to express our gratitude to Janet Aitchison for her enthusiastic commitment to the book.

*There is a satisfactory boniness about grammar which the flesh of sheer vocabulary requires before it can become vertebrate and walk the earth.*
-Anthony Burgess

Printing (last digit): 10 9 8 7 6 5 4 3 2

Printed in China

# Table of Contents

# Introduction

*Grammar Activities* for *The Oxford Picture Dictionary* enables teachers to incorporate effective beginning-level grammar practice into their lessons with *The Oxford Picture Dictionary*. Research shows that contextualized grammar instruction helps non-native speakers learn, retain, and use grammatical structures successfully.[1] Because each topic in the *Dictionary* creates a vivid context, *The Oxford Picture Dictionary* is an excellent resource for teaching grammar. Context alone, however, does not give ESL students what they need to "own" a target grammar structure. Students need extensive practice with a new structure and the opportunity to test it out in the safety of the classroom before taking it into the world. *Grammar Activities* provides a wealth of guided practice activities that develop the ability of beginning-level students to use the language they have learned.

## WHAT'S IN *GRAMMAR ACTIVITIES*?

*Grammar Activities* is divided into two sections: Teacher's Notes and Grammar Activities.

### Teacher's Notes

The Teachers' Notes show how to use the eleven different activity types featured in the Grammar Activities section. Each Note explains the purpose of the activity, strategies for presenting the target grammar, and step-by-step directions for conducting the activity. Also included are tips for adapting the activity type for use with multilevel classes.

Each activity type focuses on one or more aspects of a target grammar structure: the endings and other markers that distinguish the structure; its meaning, its written form, its use in questions and answers, and so on. The activity types are designed to appeal to students with a wide range of abilities and learning styles (e.g., kinesthetic, auditory, and visual). They can also be used to facilitate pair work as well as small-group and whole-class instruction. In addition, care has been taken to integrate a number of skills into each activity type (e.g., speaking/listening, listening/writing, reading/writing.)

For an overview of these eleven activity types, see the chart on page 1.

### Grammar Activities

This section contains 128 ready-made grammar activities that are based on the activity types introduced in the Teacher's Notes. Each activity is correlated to a topic in the *Dictionary* and practices a grammar point that is naturally related to the topic. For example, the grammar focus for *Containers and Packaged Foods* is count and noncount nouns, while the focus for *Describing Clothes* is adjective order. Working with both vocabulary and grammar in context context helps students retain what they learn. By combining pattern practice with realistic language in context, these activities build students' accuracy and fluency.

## HOW TO USE *GRAMMAR ACTIVITIES*

Grammar and vocabulary are tools we use to construct meaningful communication. Effective lesson planning includes determining the communication goal that becomes the lesson objective and then identifying the grammatical forms and vocabulary needed to attain that objective.

To create successful lessons using *Grammar Activities*, you can use any of the following methods:

- Identify the target grammar and vocabulary that support your lesson objective. Select a related topic in *The Oxford Picture Dictionary*. Then refer to the Teachers' Notes to choose and plan an activity to practice the target grammar.

OR

- Choose the activity from the Grammar Activities section that correlates to the page you're using in the *Dictionary*. Then refer to the Teacher's Notes for suggestions on how to prepare for, conduct, and follow up the activity.

OR

[1]Petrovitz, W. *The role of context in the presentation of grammar.* ELT Journal, Volume 51, Issue 3: July 1997; Hinkle, E. *New Perspectives on Teaching Grammar.* Lawrence Erlbaun Associates, 2001.

- Identify a grammar structure that students need to review. Then look up the structure in the Grammar Index to locate one or more activities that work with that structure.

## INTEGRATING GRAMMAR INSTRUCTION INTO THE LESSON

### The Introduction and Presentation Stages

Before you begin presenting a lesson, you'll want to find out what students already know about the lesson topic, the vocabulary, and the target grammar structure. Brainstorming activities can effectively assess these lesson elements. Students at all levels can work together to respond to a level-appropriate prompt such as *Label as many places on this sheet as you can* (Newcomer), or *Name all the places you know near our school* (Beginning Low), or *Write the ways to ask for directions* (Beginning High). This type of assessment activity provides you with information to use during your lesson and motivates students to focus on the presentation of new information.

There are many strategies for presenting the vocabulary, grammar structures, and concepts students will need to achieve the lesson objective. Some of the most popular methods are:

- Using pictures from *The Oxford Picture Dictionary* or other source to provide a context for the target grammar;
- Telling a story that integrates the new vocabulary and target grammar;
- Asking questions that prompt the use of the new vocabulary and grammar.

### Presenting the Target Grammar

During the presentation stage, students often work with the target grammar structure under the teacher's guidance. But the question arises: What form should this guidance take? Should students see a chart that explicitly states the form of the target grammar? Or should they learn the grammar implicitly from embedded examples in a conversation, listening passage, or reading? For beginning-level students, we believe that both types of grammar presentation are helpful when done in context and followed by sufficient practice (both guided and less-guided).

Explicit instruction points out, often in chart form, how a structure is constructed. At the beginning level, it's important to keep the chart simple and contextualized. In this way, students can focus on learning the form. From a chart, students can learn how the target grammar structure responds to number, time, and gender. An explicit presentation can be followed by guided practice activities in which examples of the grammar are embedded in meaningful communication. (See, for example, TPR Grammar, page 4, or Back and Forth, page 14.)

Implicit instruction, or presenting a structure within real-life discourse, allows students to focus on the overall meaning of the language before breaking it down to examine its form. An implicit grammar presentation employs visual and contextual support to ensure students' comprehension and encourages students to identify the purpose of the message. To be sure that students understand the form of the target grammar, an implicit presentation can be followed by a guided practice activity that focuses on constructing the target grammar. (See, for example, Mark My Words, page 9, or Sentence Maker, page 12.)

Discovery is another presentation strategy that can be adapted for use at the beginning level.[2] In this type of presentation, students see a number of contextualized sentences that illustrate the target grammar structure. The teacher verifies comprehension of the sentences and then elicits from the class the similarities and differences in the sentences. As the teacher marks the sentences according to students' comments and lists similarities and differences on the board, students begin to "discover" the grammar formula. The teacher then elicits additional sentences that follow that formula and gives any level-appropriate exceptions.

[2] Fotos, Sandra and Ellis, Rod. *Communicating about Grammar: A Task Based Approach.* TESOL Quarterly. Vol. 25, No. 4 Winter 1991.

No matter which presentation strategy you choose, remember to ask students to demonstrate their comprehension of what you have presented by having them respond to commands or answer questions about the lesson content.

## Moving from Guided to Less-Guided Practice

The guided practice activities in *Grammar Activities* are highly interactive and provide practice with the patterns that students will use in their communication outside the classroom. Each activity is carefully structured for success so that students become more confident and can begin to take risks in less-guided and more communicative practice activities (e.g., working together to make a simple community directory or role-playing to ask for and give directions.) With this in mind, *Grammar Activities* can be used as an introduction to more communicative activities, such as those found in *The Oxford Picture Dictionary Teacher's Book* and *Classic Classroom Activities*. Like *Grammar Activities*, both of these *Dictionary* components offer activities for each topic in the *Dictionary*.

We hope you enjoy using *The Grammar Activity Book* and that it becomes a springboard for creating additional grammar lessons using *The Oxford Picture Dictionary*. We invite you to write us with your comments at:

English Language Teaching Division
Oxford University Press
198 Madison Avenue
New York, NY 10016

*Jayme Adelson-Goldstein & Norma Shapiro*

# Teacher's Notes

## OVERVIEW

| ACTIVITY TYPES | PAGE | SKILLS | GROUPING | DESCRIPTION |
|---|---|---|---|---|
| **ANSWERS UP*** | **2** | Listening | Whole Class | Students hold up flash cards to indicate which grammatical markers they hear. |
| **PEER DICTATION** | **3** | Listening<br>Speaking<br>Reading<br>Writing | Pairs | Pairs dictate, clarify, and write sentences that use the target grammar. |
| **TPR GRAMMAR*** | **4** | Listening<br>Speaking | Whole Class | Students follow Total Physical Response commands and respond to questions that elicit the target grammar. |
| **CLASS GO-AROUND** | **5** | Listening<br>Speaking | Whole Class | Using the target grammar and vocabulary, students add items to a chain drill. |
| **BOARD RACE** | **6** | Listening<br>Reading<br>Writing | Large Teams | Teams race to write answers to questions using the target grammar. |
| **AROUND THE TABLE** | **7** | Listening<br>Speaking | Small Groups | Small groups conduct question-and-answer drills that illustrate the target grammar. |
| **TIC-TAC-TOE** | **8** | Listening<br>Speaking | Two Teams | Two teams ask and answer questions using the target grammar. |
| **MARK MY WORDS** | **9** | Listening<br>Speaking<br>Reading<br>Writing | Large Teams | Teams take turns marking corrections in sentences that illustrate the target grammar. |
| **INTERVIEW** | **10-11** | Reading<br>Writing | Pairs | Pairs ask and answer questions that employ the target grammar and then write complete answers on a worksheet. |
| **SENTENCE MAKER*** | **12-13** | Listening<br>Speaking<br>Reading<br>Writing | Small Groups | Using word cards, small groups create and write meaningful sentences and questions with the target grammar and vocabulary. |
| **BACK AND FORTH** | **14** | Listening<br>Speaking | Pairs or Triads | Pairs or triads work with a dialogue that incorporates the target grammar and then adjust the vocabulary and situation to create their own role play. |

*While all the grammar activities can be used with beginning-level students, those that are starred work especially well for students with little prior education.

# ANSWERS UP

| Literacy to Beginning High | |
|---|---|
| Whole Class | |
| Preparation: | 10 minutes |
| Activity: | 15 minutes |

**Objective:** Using flash cards, students will be able to demonstrate understanding of differences in word forms, intonation, tenses, or other sentence elements.

**Preparation:** Preview the statements from the selected Answers Up activity.

***OR*** Using vocabulary from the selected dictionary page, write eight to ten statements that practice the target grammar structure.

On the board, write the words or symbols students will use on their flash cards. Give students index cards (or 3″ x 5″ pieces of paper) and help them write the words or symbols in large, bold print on their cards. Make a set of oversize cards for yourself on 8½″ x 11″ paper.

## REVIEW THE VOCABULARY

Have students point to the items on the dictionary page as you name them (e.g., *He's a man. She's a woman.*).

## TEACH THE GRAMMAR POINT

Call students' attention to the target grammar structure by charting its form on the board or on an overhead transparency. Then identify its meaning and/or use.

## INTRODUCE THE ACTIVITY

Explain the goal: for students to listen and identify what they hear by holding up the correct card.

## MODEL AND CONDUCT THE ACTIVITY

1. Make your first statement and hold up the correct oversize card. Make another statement and have the class tell you which card to hold up.
2. Make your next statement and have students use their own cards. Continue. Re-use the statements you have modeled, if desired.

## SAMPLE ACTIVITY

### Age and Physical Description (Dictionary, p. 22)

**NOUNS: SINGULAR AND PLURAL**
*He's a tall man. They're short men.*

Make each statement below. Have students indicate whether they heard a singular or plural noun by holding up the card labeled "1" (for singular) or "2+" (for plural).

1. He's a tall man.
2. They're short men.
3. They're adults.
4. Look at these babies!
5. She's an attractive woman.
6. I see a six-year-old boy.
7. He's a cute baby.
8. Look at those girls.

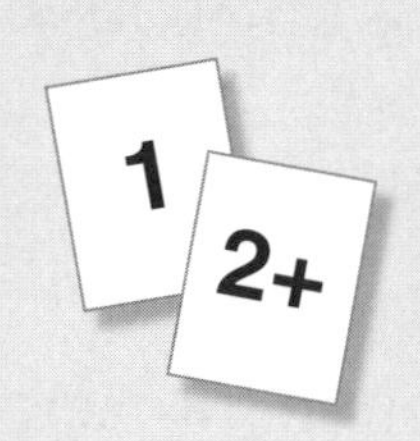


### For Multilevel Classes

Follow up by having pairs of higher-level students work together to create four to six new sentences similar to those in the activity, while lower-level students copy the original sentences. Then have each pair of higher-level students conduct an Answers Up activity with a pair of lower-level students.

## PEER DICTATION

| Beginning Low to Beginning High |
| --- |
| Pairs |
| Preparation: 5 minutes |
| Activity: 10–15 minutes |

**Objective:** Students will be able to listen to their partners dictate statements, to ask for clarification of what they hear, and to write what they hear accurately.

**Preparation:** Preview the statements in the selected Peer Dictation activity.

***OR*** Using vocabulary from the selected dictionary page, create four to six sentences that practice the target grammar structure.

Write the sentences on the board or on an overhead transparency, and conceal them from the class. On a piece of paper, write a model sentence for Student A to dictate to Student B. On another piece of paper, write a sentence for Student B to dictate to Student A.

### REVIEW THE VOCABULARY

Have students dictate target vocabulary words to you. Model clarification strategies by interrupting students to ask for repetition or spelling.

### TEACH THE GRAMMAR POINT

Write two to three sentences on the board that illustrate the target grammar structure. Ask students to circle the parts of the sentence that show the structure.

### INTRODUCE THE ACTIVITY

Explain the goal: for students to listen to their partners and write what they hear.

### MODEL AND CONDUCT THE ACTIVITY

1. Write one or more clarification questions on the board (e.g., *Could you repeat that? How do you spell...? Did you say...?*). Practice with the class.
2. Have two students come to the board. Assign one role A, and assign the other role B. Ask Student A to dictate the model sentence to Student B. Encourage Student B to ask for clarification before she/he writes the sentence on the board. Then have Student B dictate the other model sentence to Student A. Have the class check the students' accuracy.
3. Pair students and assign A/B roles. Have pairs sit so that Student A can see the sentences, but Student B cannot. Reveal the A sentences on the board or on the overhead transparency. Have Student A dictate the sentences to Student B. Set a four-minute time limit.
4. Call time and have partners switch seats. Reveal the B sentences and have Student B dictate the sentences to Student A. Set a time limit. Have partners check each other's work.

### SAMPLE ACTIVITY

#### Numbers and Measurements

(Dictionary, pp. 14–15)

**SIMPLE PRESENT**

*12 inches equal 1 foot. I yard equals 3 feet.*

Write the sentences below on the board or on an overhead transparency, and conceal them from the class. Present the clarification strategy: *Did you say...?* Pair students and assign A/B roles. (Have students sit so that the student who is dictating can see the sentences, but the one who is writing cannot.) Student A dictates first, and then Student B. Have partners check each other's work.

**A Sentences**

1. 1,760 yards equal 1 mile.
2. 1 inch equals 2.54 centimeters.
3. 1 yard equals 3 feet.
4. 75% equals 3/4.

**B Sentences**

1. 1.6 kilometers equal 1 mile.
2. 1 yard equals .91 meters.
3. 12 inches equal 1 foot.
4. 1/2 equals 50%.

### For Multilevel Classes

Adjust the level of the A sentences to match that of lower-level students. Adjust the level of the B sentences to match that of higher-level students. Pair higher- and lower-level students. Have higher-level partners dictate the A sentences and lower-level partners dictate the B sentences.

## TPR GRAMMAR

| Literacy to Beginning High |
|---|
| Whole Class |
| Preparation: 10 minutes |
| Activity: 15 minutes |

**Objective:** Students will be able to use verb forms accurately when responding to questions about a Total Physical Response (TPR) sequence.

**Preparation:** Preview the selected TPR Grammar activity.

***OR*** Using the TPR sequence on the selected dictionary page, create follow-up questions that practice the target grammar structure.

Collect any picture cards or props you think will be helpful.

---

### REVIEW THE VOCABULARY

Review each command from the dictionary page. Give the commands without demonstrating them, and have students perform the actions. Then invite students to command you. Make mistakes so students can correct you.

### TEACH THE GRAMMAR POINT

Using the vocabulary from the dictionary page, make statements that use the target form (e.g., *I'm picking up the receiver. Now I'm listening for the dial tone.*).

Draw a chart on the board that shows the verb form for each pronoun.

### INTRODUCE THE ACTIVITY

Explain the goal: to practice talking about events in the present or other time period.

### MODEL AND CONDUCT THE ACTIVITY

1. Ask a student volunteer to act out one of the actions from the sequence. Then describe the action, using the target form.
2. Have other students, individually and in groups, act out other actions so that the class uses a variety of pronouns to respond to your questions.
3. Command individuals and groups to perform various actions. Ask the class questions that will elicit statements using the target form.

### SAMPLE ACTIVITY

**The Telephone** (Dictionary, p. 9)

**PRESENT CONTINUOUS**

*He's picking up the receiver.*

Command individuals and groups to perform the actions below. While students are performing each action, ask the class the questions to elicit present continuous statements.

| Teacher Commands | Teacher Questions |
|---|---|
| Pick up the receiver. | What's he doing? |
| Listen for the dial tone. | What's she doing? |
| Deposit 25 cents. | What are they doing? |
| Dial 555-0470. | What are you doing? |
| Leave a message. | What am I doing? |
| Hang up the receiver. | What is she doing? |

### For Multilevel Classes

Have literacy students and newcomers respond nonverbally to the commands. Have students with stronger skills practice producing the target grammar structure in response to your questions.

## CLASS GO-AROUND

| Beginning Low to Beginning High |
|---|
| Whole Class |
| Preparation: 3 minutes |
| Activity: 10 minutes |

**Objective:** Using a chain drill, students will be able to recall and create sentences that use the target grammar structure and vocabulary.

**Preparation:** Preview the selected Class Go-Around activity.

***OR*** Identify a target structure that you want students to practice with the vocabulary from the selected dictionary page. Create a model sentence that demonstrates the structure.

### REVIEW THE VOCABULARY

Say a topic word from the dictionary. Have a student repeat the word and add another one. Have students take turns repeating and adding words. When students can't think of any more topic words, write the words on the board and review the meanings.

### TEACH THE GRAMMAR POINT

Put an example of the target grammar structure (e.g., *There is/There are*) on the board. Give its meaning and/or use. Have students look at the selected dictionary page as you make sentences that use the target structure. Write the sentences on the board.

### INTRODUCE THE ACTIVITY

Explain the goal: for students to remember the sentences they hear, repeat them, and add a new sentence.

### MODEL AND CONDUCT THE ACTIVITY

1. Model a chain drill. Have one student say the first sentence on the board. Have another student repeat that sentence and add the next sentence. Continue until students have said all the sentences. Then erase the board.
2. Start the chain drill by saying one of the sentences students practiced. Have a student repeat your sentence and add another sentence. Continue the chain with at least five more students, each one repeating what has been said and adding a new sentence.

### SAMPLE ACTIVITY

#### A Dining Area (Dictionary, p. 41)

**NOUNS: SINGULAR AND PLURAL; *THERE IS/ THERE ARE***

*There are five place mats, and there's one teapot.*

Have students look at the dictionary page as you identify the name and quantity of some of the items in the dining room. Start the chain drill by saying the first sentence below. Have a student repeat what you've said and add another object. Continue the chain with at least five more students, each one repeating what has been said and adding another object.

**T:** There are five place mats in this dining room.
**S1:** There are five place mats, and there's one teapot in this dining room.
**S2:** There are five place mats, there's one teapot, and there are two candlesticks in this dining room.

### For Multilevel Classes

Do two rounds of this activity: one for the whole class and one for groups. Have higher-level students participate in round 1. In round 2, have higher-level groups see how long they can continue the chain in their groups. Have lower-level groups try to finish at least one chain.

## BOARD RACE

| Beginning Low to Beginning High |
|---|
| Large Teams |
| Preparation: 10 minutes |
| Activity: 15–20 minutes |

**Objective:** Working in teams, students will be able to find the answer to a question and write the answer correctly.

**Preparation:** Preview the questions in the selected Board Race activity.

***OR*** Using the vocabulary from the selected dictionary page, write six to eight questions whose answers incorporate the target grammar structure.

### REVIEW THE VOCABULARY

Ask questions with *or,* using the vocabulary from the dictionary page (e.g., *Is she looking at a purse or shoes?),* and have students respond in complete sentences (e.g., *She's looking at a purse.).*

### TEACH THE GRAMMAR POINT

Use the language from the vocabulary review to call out and explain the target grammar (e.g., *She's looking at a purse.*).

### INTRODUCE THE ACTIVITY

Explain the goal: to listen to each question and work with teammates to find and write the answer on the board.

### MODEL AND CONDUCT THE ACTIVITY

1. Divide the class into large teams of eight to ten students. Have students look at the selected dictionary page. Model the activity by asking the first question from the activity. Give students one minute to work together to find the correct answer and write it on the board. Monitor and assist as needed.
2. Call time and check answers. Ask the class to identify the correct answers. Elicit corrections for incorrect answers.
3. Tell students they will hear five more questions and will get 1 point for each correct answer. Begin the activity by asking the second question from the activity.

### SAMPLE ACTIVITY

**Shoes and Accessories** (Dictionary, pp. 68–69)

**PRESENT CONTINUOUS: STATEMENTS**
*She's looking at a purse. He's trying on shoes.*

Ask the questions below. Have teams check the dictionary page and race to write the complete answers on the board.

| What is the… | Answers |
|---|---|
| 1. woman in the green sweater doing? | 1. She's looking at a purse. |
| 2. woman in the yellow sweater doing? | 2. She's trying on a silk scarf. |
| 3. woman in the purple sweater doing? | 3. She's showing a watch. |
| 4. woman in the pink suit doing? | 4. She's looking at the watch. |
| 5. man in the suspenders doing? | 5. He's waiting in line. |
| 6. man in blue jeans doing? | 6. He's trying on shoes. |
| 7. woman in the orange sweater doing? | 7. She's taking the bag. |
| 8. woman in the blue and white dress doing? | 8. She's waiting in line. |

### For Multilevel Classes

Prepare a handout with the answers to your questions. Create mixed-level teams of beginning-low and beginning-high students. While the teams are finding the correct answers, have literacy-level students copy the answers from the handout into their notebooks and then help correct the answers on the board.

## AROUND THE TABLE

| Literacy to Beginning High |
| --- |
| Small Groups |
| Preparation: 5 minutes |
| Activity: 10 minutes |

**Objective:** Students will be able to conduct a question and answer (Q&A) or substitution drill that practices the target grammar structure(s) and vocabulary.

**Preparation:** Preview the Q&A or substitution drill in the selected Around the Table activity.

***OR*** Create one or two questions for students to use in a Q&A drill. The questions should prompt the use of the target grammar structure(s) and the vocabulary from the selected dictionary page.

### REVIEW THE VOCABULARY

Check comprehension of key vocabulary by giving a definition and having students call out the word or phrase.

### TEACH THE GRAMMAR POINT

Write the first drill question and a possible answer (or the first statement and a possible substitution) on the board. Show students (or elicit from them) how the elements of the question and answer, or statements, relate. For example:

What's that? It's a pencil.

I like oranges. I like apples.

### INTRODUCE THE ACTIVITY

Explain the goal: to practice asking and answering questions or making statements in groups of four.

### MODEL AND CONDUCT THE ACTIVITY

1. Conduct the Q&A (or substitution) drill with the whole class. Ask the drill question (e.g., *What's that?*), and write it on the board. Have one student answer (*It's a…*). Instruct the student to ask another classmate the question. (For a substitution drill, make a statement and have another student make the same statement but substitute different information.)
2. Demonstrate the group drill. Assign roles A through D to four students. Have Student A start by asking Student B the question or making the statement. Have students go "around the table" asking and answering questions or making statements.
3. Form groups of four students and assign roles A through D in each group. Have students conduct the drill. Set a time limit of three to four minutes.
4. Call time and present the second drill, if there is one.

### SAMPLE ACTIVITY

**A Classroom** (Dictionary, pp. 2–3)

***THIS/THAT*; QUESTIONS AND ANSWERS**
*What's that? Is this your pen?*

Practice the question-and-answer (Q&A) forms. Form groups of four students and assign roles A through D in each group. Have students conduct the Q&A drills.

**Round 1: *Wh-* Questions**
Student A: *(pointing to B's pencil)* What's that?
Student B: It's a pencil. *(pointing to a map)* What's that?
Student C: It's a map. *(pointing to D's notebook)* What's that?
Student D: It's a notebook. *(pointing to A's pen)* What's that?
Etc.

**Round 2: *Yes/No* Questions**
Student A: *(touching C's pencil)* Is this your pencil?
Student B: No, it isn't. *(pointing to C's pen)* Is that your pen?
Student C: Yes, it is. *(touching D's book)* Is this your book?
Etc.

### For Multilevel Classes

Create groups with students of similar abilities. Have higher-level students try to go around the table at least twice. Have lower-levels students try to go around the table at least once.

# TIC-TAC-TOE

| Beginning Low to Beginning High |
|---|
| Two Teams |
| Preparation: 5 minutes |
| Activity: 10 minutes |

**Objective:** Students will be able to ask and answer questions accurately.

**Preparation:** Preview the grid(s) and prompt(s) from the selected Tic-Tac-Toe activity and copy the grid onto the board or an overhead transparency.

***OR*** Create Tic-Tac-Toe cues using the vocabulary on the selected dictionary page. Cues should prompt students to create statements or questions that practice the target grammar structure. Draw the grid on the board or an overhead transparency.

## REVIEW THE VOCABULARY

Make statements about the dictionary picture and have students identify whether the statements are true or false (e.g., *The clerk is in the library.* False; *The students are in the auditorium.* True.).

## TEACH THE GRAMMAR POINT

Present examples of the statements or questions students will be making during the activity. Demonstrate or elicit from the class how to form similar types of statements or questions.

## INTRODUCE THE ACTIVITY

Explain the goal: to play a Tic-Tac-Toe game to practice making statements or asking and answering questions.

## MODEL AND CONDUCT THE ACTIVITY

1. Draw a blank Tic-Tac-Toe grid on the board or an overhead transparency and survey the class to find out how many students know how to play the game. Play a sample game with a student to demonstrate.
2. Divide the class into two teams: X and O. Have students on each team choose a leader.
3. Use the Tic-Tac-Toe grid on the board or overhead transparency. Determine which team will go first. Have the leader from the first team choose a square (e.g., upper-left: *counselor*). Give the prompt (e.g., *Where's the counselor?*), and allow 30 seconds for the team leader to get input from the team. Call time and have the team leader give the answer. If the answer is correct, the team gets the square. If not, the square is still in play.

## SAMPLE ACTIVITY

### School (Dictionary, p. 5)

***WH-* QUESTIONS: *WHERE IS/ARE...?*;**
**PREPOSITIONS OF PLACE: *IN***

*Where is the counselor? She's in the counselor's office.*

Copy the Tic-Tac-Toe grid onto the board or an overhead transparency. Play the game, using the suggested prompt.

| | | |
|---|---|---|
| counselor | lockers | clerk |
| principal | chalkboard | coach |
| teacher | hungry students | books |

**Round 1**

Prompt: *Where is/are the...?*

Students respond with *He's/She's/It's/They're in the...*, based on the pictures in the dictionary.

**Round 2**

Students on the same team ask and answer the question *Where is/are the...?*

### For Multilevel Classes

Make a copy of the Tic-Tac-Toe grid for each group of five to seven students. Have one higher-level student run the game for four to six lower-level students.

## MARK MY WORDS

| Beginning Low to Beginning High |
|---|
| Large Teams |
| Preparation: 5 minutes |
| Activity: 15 minutes |

**Objective:** Students will be able to identify and correct errors in sentences that use the target grammar structure and vocabulary.

**Preparation:** Preview the sentences in the selected Mark My Words activity.

***OR*** Using vocabulary from the selected dictionary page, create five to eight sentences, most of which should contain an error in the target grammar structure.

Write the sentences on the board or on an overhead transparency and conceal them from the class.

### REVIEW THE VOCABULARY

Write five to ten target words from the dictionary page on the board, misspelling the majority of them. Have students look in their dictionaries to find the correct spellings. Then elicit the meaning of each word.

### TEACH THE GRAMMAR POINT

Write sentences on the board that illustrate the target grammar point. Show students (or elicit from them) the structural similarities in the sentences.

### INTRODUCE THE ACTIVITY

Explain the goal: to find and correct mistakes in different sentences.

### MODEL AND CONDUCT THE ACTIVITY

1. Write a sentence on the board that incorrectly describes a person, item, or location from the selected dictionary page.
2. Have students look in their dictionaries and tell you the error. Ask a student to come to the board and correct the sentence. Check with the class to see if all students agree with the correction.
3. Divide the class into four teams: A, B, C, and D. Reveal the sentences on the board or overhead transparency. Have students look at the dictionary picture to determine which sentences contain a mistake and which are correct, according to the picture.
4. Have students from different teams take turns circling the errors and writing the correct sentences. Ask the class to say whether the new sentences are accurate.

### SAMPLE ACTIVITY

**A Bathroom** (Dictionary, p. 43)

**PREPOSITIONS OF PLACE: *NEXT TO, IN FRONT OF, ABOVE, UNDER, IN, ON, ACROSS FROM***
*The hamper is next to the tub.*

Write the sentences below on the board. Have students look at the dictionary picture to determine which sentences contain a mistake and which are correct. Then have teams take turns circling the errors and writing the correct sentences.

1. The hamper is across from the tub.
2. The mother and child are under the bath mat.
3. The scale is in front of the wastebasket.
4. The blue towels are above the window.
5. The toothbrushes are in the sink.
6. The rubber mat is next to the tub.
7. The medicine cabinet is above the sink.
8. The soap is next to the soap dish.

**Corrections: 1.** next to; **2.** on; **3.** OK; **4.** under; **5.** on; **6.** in; **7.** OK; **8.** on

### For Multilevel Classes

Have lower-level students copy the eight correct sentences from the board. Have higher-level students work together to write new sentences that use the target structure.

## INTERVIEW

| Beginning Low to Beginning High |
| --- |
| Pairs |
| Preparation: 5 minutes |
| Activity: 15 minutes |

**Objective:** Students will be able to ask and answer questions and then practice the target structure by writing their answers and their partners' answers.

**Preparation:** Make one copy of the Interview worksheet on p. 11. Write the questions from the selected Interview activity in section A of the worksheet.

***OR*** Using vocabulary from the selected dictionary page, create four questions that practice the target grammar structure. Write these questions in section A of the Interview worksheet.

In sections B and C, write examples of complete sentences based on the Interview responses. For B, write a sentence in the first person (e.g., *I wake up at 7:00 A.M.*). For C, write a sentence in the third person (e.g., *Maria wakes up at 6:30 A.M.*). Duplicate a class set of the worksheet and copy it onto the board or an overhead transparency.

### REVIEW THE VOCABULARY

Ask questions about the dictionary picture (e.g., *Does he eat breakfast at . . . ? Does he go to school or watch TV at . . . ?*).

### TEACH THE GRAMMAR POINT

Ask two of the Interview questions, and write the answers on the board. Explain the target structure, or have students create new questions and answers that show they understand it.

### INTRODUCE THE ACTIVITY

Explain the goal: for students to find out about their partners by asking and answering questions and to practice writing answers.

### MODEL AND CONDUCT THE ACTIVITY

1. Ask yourself the Interview questions aloud, and write your short answers on the worksheet you have copied on the board or overhead transparency.
2. Interview a student and write his/her short answers on the board or on an overhead transparency.
3. Pair students. Have them write their own short answers on their worksheets first. Then have them interview their partners and write their partners' short answers.
4. Have students write the follow-up sentences in sections B and C independently while you monitor and offer assistance.

### SAMPLE ACTIVITY

**Daily Routines** (Dictionary, pp. 26–27)

**SIMPLE PRESENT**

*What time do you wake up? I wake up at 6:00 A.M.*

Copy the questions (or the alternative questions) below on a copy of the Interview worksheet (p. 11). Follow the directions on the worksheet to have pairs write their own short answers and then their partners' short answers. Have students write follow-up sentences based on the interview answers.

| Interview Questions | Alternative Questions |
| --- | --- |
| 1. What time do you wake up? | 1. Do you make your lunch or buy it? |
| 2. What time do you eat breakfast? | 2. Do you watch TV at night? |
| 3. What time do you go to school? | 3. Do you exercise? When? |
| 4. What time do you eat lunch? | 4. What time do you go to sleep? |

### For Multilevel Classes

Pair literacy-level students or newcomers with beginning-high students. Have pairs share a worksheet. Have the beginning-high students write the follow-up sentences while partners help.

## INTERVIEW WORKSHEET

**A.** Write your short answers to the questions.
Then interview your partner and write his/her short answers.

| Interview questions | My answers | My partner's answers |
|---|---|---|
| **1.** | | |
| **2.** | | |
| **3.** | | |
| **4.** | | |

**B.** Write about yourself.

**Example:** ____________________

| |
|---|
| **1.** |
| **2.** |
| **3.** |
| **4.** |

**C.** Write about your partner.

**Example:** ____________________

| |
|---|
| **1.** |
| **2.** |
| **3.** |
| **4.** |

## SENTENCE MAKER

| Beginning Low to Beginning High |
| --- |
| Small Groups |
| Preparation: 15 minutes |
| Activity: 20 minutes |

**Objective:** Using word cards, students will be able to create meaningful, accurate sentences and questions that use the target grammar structure and vocabulary.

**Preparation:** Make one copy of the Sentence Maker grid on p. 13. Copy the 18 words or phrases from the selected Sentence Maker activity onto the cards.

***OR*** Choose 18 words or phrases from the selected dictionary page. Students will use these words to make sentences and questions that practice the target grammar structure. Write the words on the Sentence Maker grid.

Duplicate and cut apart one set of word cards for each group of four to six students. Create ten large word cards to use in the model. Use the following words: *He/is/a/Is/student/teacher/good/he/./?/*

### REVIEW THE VOCABULARY

On the board, write cloze sentences based on the dictionary topic (e.g., *That __ a __ car. ____ is a __ chair.*). Have students look at the selected dictionary page and use the vocabulary to fill in the blanks.

### TEACH THE GRAMMAR POINT

Have students find the similarities in the cloze sentences. Point out that the similarities are examples of the target grammar structure. Elicit additional sentences that illustrate the target structure.

### INTRODUCE THE ACTIVITY

Explain the goal: to use the word cards to make sentences and questions.

### MODEL AND CONDUCT THE ACTIVITY

1. Place the ten large word cards on the chalk tray. Elicit and write on the board sentences and questions based on the word cards. Make mistakes as you write (e.g., in word order or capitalization), and have the class correct you.
2. Put students into groups. Distribute one set of 20 cards (18 word cards and the cards with "." and "?") to each group. Have each group choose a recorder.
3. Direct students to make one sentence or question with some of the cards, and have the recorder write it down on a separate sheet of paper. Check accuracy.
4. Have groups continue making and recording sentences and questions. Monitor their work and give feedback on their accuracy. Set a ten-minute time limit, and then have groups report back on one or more of their sentences and questions.

### SAMPLE ACTIVITY

**Describing Things** (Dictionary, p. 11)

**ADJECTIVE ORDER; *THIS/THAT***

*This is an expensive chair. That chair is cheap.*

Write the words below on a copy of the Sentence Maker grid (p. 12). Duplicate and cut apart one set of word cards for each group of four to six students. Have each group use their cards to make sentences or questions, while a group recorder writes them on a separate sheet of paper. Instruct students to make and record as many sentences or questions as they can.

| | | | | | |
| --- | --- | --- | --- | --- | --- |
| This | That | is | isn't | light | chair |
| a | an | good | expensive | book | car |
| cheap | heavy | hard | soft | Is | this |

### For Multilevel Classes

Group higher- and lower-level students together. Have a higher-level student be the recorder, and have a lower-level student report back to the class.

## SENTENCE MAKER GRID

| | | | |
|---|---|---|---|
| | | | |
| | | | |
| | | | |
| | | | |
| | | ? | . |

## BACK AND FORTH

| Beginning Low to Beginning High |
| --- |
| Pairs or Triads |
| Preparation: 10 minutes |
| Activity: 15 minutes |

**Objective:** Students will be able to use the target grammar structure and vocabulary to role-play a conversation.

**Preparation:** Preview the conversation from the selected Back and Forth activity.

***OR*** Using the vocabulary from the selected dictionary page, write a conversation that practices the target grammar structure.

### REVIEW THE VOCABULARY

Have students open their dictionaries to the selected page and cover the word list. Have students work in groups of two or three and take turns asking each other to name items on the page.

### TEACH THE GRAMMAR POINT

Present the sentences from the conversation that best illustrate the target grammar structure. Ask *True/False* questions about the meanings of the sentences to verify understanding of the form and meaning of the structure.

### INTRODUCE THE ACTIVITY

Explain the goal: to practice a conversation and then create a new one.

### MODEL AND CONDUCT THE ACTIVITY

1. Put the model conversation on the board. Introduce the situation and role-play the conversation with volunteers.
2. Ask the class *Yes/No* questions to verify that students understand what they are saying.
3. Have students form groups of two or three and practice the conversation. Encourage students to substitute their own information and/or use their imaginations to change the location or situation.
4. Invite groups to role-play their conversations for the class. Give the class specific information to listen for (e.g., *How do they feel? Who do they meet?*).

### SAMPLE ACTIVITY

**Everyday Conversation** (Dictionary, p. 8)

**SIMPLE PRESENT: *BE***
*I'm Ana.*

Put the model conversation on the board. Introduce the situation and role-play the conversation with volunteers. Have students form groups of three and role-play their own version of the conversation.

Ana and Cara walk up to a student at a party.

**Ana:** Hi, I'm Ana.
**Cara:** And I'm Cara.
**Bob:** Nice to meet you. I'm Bob *(coughs)*.
**Cara:** Nice to meet you too.
*(to Ana)* What's his name?
**Ana:** *(to Cara)* I'm not sure.
*(to Bob)* Did you say Bob?
**Bob:** Yes, I'm Bob.
**Cara and Ana:** Nice to meet you, Bob.

### For Multilevel Classes

After you have presented the target grammar structure and the conversation, have lower-level students work in groups of two or three to practice the conversations. With higher-level students, brainstorm situations in which people would use the target sentences. Then observe the lower-level groups role-playing their conversations while the higher-level students write their own conversations. Finally, have the higher-level students role-play their conversations for the class.

# Grammar Activities

## A Classroom (Dictionary, pp. 2–3)

### IMPERATIVES

**Tic-Tac-Toe**
Teacher's Notes, p. 8

*Put away your pencil. Raise your hand.*

Copy the Tic-Tac-Toe grid onto the board or an overhead transparency. Play the game, using the suggested prompt.

| put away | open | raise |
|---|---|---|
| listen to | point to | erase |
| close | write | take out |

Prompt: *Tell a teammate to [do something].*
Students respond by giving and acting out the complete commands, based on the pictures in the dictionary.

### *THIS/THAT;* SIMPLE PRESENT: QUESTIONS AND ANSWERS

**Around the Table**
Teacher's Notes, p. 7

*What's that? Is this your pen?*

Practice the question-and-answer (Q&A) forms. Form groups of four students and assign roles A through D in each group. Have students conduct the Q&A drills.

**Round 1:** ***Wh-* Questions**
Student A: *(pointing to B's pencil)* What's that?
Student B: It's a pencil. *(pointing to a map)* What's that?
Student C: It's a map. *(pointing to D's notebook)* What's that?
Student D: It's a notebook. *(pointing to A's pen)* What's that?
Etc.

**Round 2:** ***Yes/No* Questions**
Student A: *(touching C's pencil)* Is this your pencil?
Student B: No, it isn't. *(pointing to C's pen)* Is that your pen?
Student C: Yes, it is. *(touching D's book)* Is this your book?
Etc.

## Personal Information (Dictionary, p. 4)

### *WH-* QUESTIONS: *WHAT*

**Interview**
Teacher's Notes, p. 10

*What is your name? What's your ZIP code?*

Copy the questions (or the alternative questions) below on a copy of the Interview worksheet (p. 11). Follow the directions on the worksheet to have pairs write their own short answers and then their partners' short answers. Have students write follow-up sentences based on the interview answers.

**Interview Questions**
1. What is your first name?
2. What is your middle name?
3. What is your last name?
4. What is your ZIP code?

**Alternative Questions**
1. What's your name?
2. What's your middle initial?
3. What street do you live on?
4. What's your date of birth?

## School (Dictionary, p. 5)

### *WH-* QUESTIONS: *WHERE IS/ARE . . . ?*; PREPOSITIONS OF PLACE: *IN*

**Tic-Tac-Toe**
Teacher's Notes, p. 8

*Where is the counselor? She's in the counselor's office.*

Copy the Tic-Tac-Toe grid onto the board or an overhead transparency. Play the game, using the suggested prompt.

| | | |
|---|---|---|
| counselor | lockers | clerk |
| principal | chalkboard | coach |
| teacher | hungry students | books |

**Round 1**
Prompt: *Where is/are the . . . ?*
Students respond with *He's/She's/It's/They're in the . . .*, based on the pictures in the dictionary.

**Round 2**
Students on the same team ask and answer the question *Where is/are the . . . ?*

## Studying (Dictionary, pp. 6–7)

### IMPERATIVES: AFFIRMATIVE AND NEGATIVE

**Answers Up**
Teacher's Notes, p. 2

*Cross out the word. Don't circle the answers.*

Give each command below. Have students indicate whether they heard an affirmative or a negative command by holding up the card labeled "DO IT" (for affirmative) or "DON'T DO IT" (for negative).

1. Cross out the word.
2. Don't circle the answers.
3. Help your partner.
4. Share your answers.
5. Don't copy them.
6. Don't discuss them.
7. Don't underline the word.
8. Dictate the word to your partner.
9. Don't repeat it.
10. Work in a group.

## Everyday Conversation (Dictionary, p. 8)

### SIMPLE PRESENT: *BE*

*I'm Ana.*

**Back and Forth**
Teacher's Notes, p. 14

Put the model conversation on the board. Introduce the situation and role-play the conversation with volunteers. Have students form groups of three and role-play their own version of the conversation.

<u>Ana</u> and <u>Cara</u> walk up to a <u>student at a party</u>.

**Ana:** Hi, I'm <u>Ana</u>.
**Cara:** And I'm <u>Cara</u>.
**Bob:** Nice to meet you. I'm <u>Bob</u> *(coughs).*
**Cara:** Nice to meet you too.
*(to Ana)* What's <u>his</u> name?
**Ana:** *(to Cara)* I'm not sure.
*(to Bob)* Did you say <u>Bob</u>?
**Bob:** Yes, I'm <u>Bob</u>.
**Cara and Ana:** Nice to meet you, <u>Bob</u>.

## The Telephone (Dictionary, p. 9)

### PRESENT CONTINUOUS

*He's picking up the receiver.*

**TPR Grammar**
Teacher's Notes, p. 4

Command individuals and groups to perform the actions below. While students are performing each action, ask the class the questions to elicit present continuous statements.

| **Teacher Commands** | **Teacher Questions** |
|---|---|
| Pick up the receiver. | What's he doing? |
| Listen for the dial tone. | What's she doing? |
| Deposit 25 cents. | What are they doing? |
| Dial 555-0470. | What are you doing? |
| Leave a message. | What am I doing? |
| Hang up the receiver. | What is she doing? |

## Weather (Dictionary, p. 10)

### SIMPLE PRESENT VS. AND SIMPLE PAST: *BE*

*It's hot. It was sunny.*

**Tic-Tac-Toe**
Teacher's Notes, p. 8

Copy the Tic-Tac-Toe grids onto the board or an overhead transparency. Play the game, using the suggested prompts.

**Round 1**
Prompt: *How's the weather?*
Students base their responses on the Fahrenheit temperature in the square (e.g., 102°: *It's hot.*).

**Round 2**
Prompt: *What was the weather like in <u>Chile</u> yesterday?*
Students base their responses on the Fahrenheit temperature in the square (e.g., *It's sunny.* or *It was sunny.*).

| | | |
|---|---|---|
| 46° | 18° | 29° |
| 75° | 60° | 0° |
| 102° | 83° | 95° |

## Describing Things (Dictionary, p. 11)

### ADJECTIVE ORDER; *THIS/THAT*

**Sentence Maker**
Teacher's Notes, p. 12

*This is an expensive chair. That chair is cheap.*

Write the words below on a copy of the Sentence Maker grid (p. 13). Duplicate and cut apart one set of word cards for each group of four to six students. Have each group use their cards to make sentences or questions, while a group recorder writes them on a separate sheet of paper. Instruct students to make and record as many sentences or questions as they can.

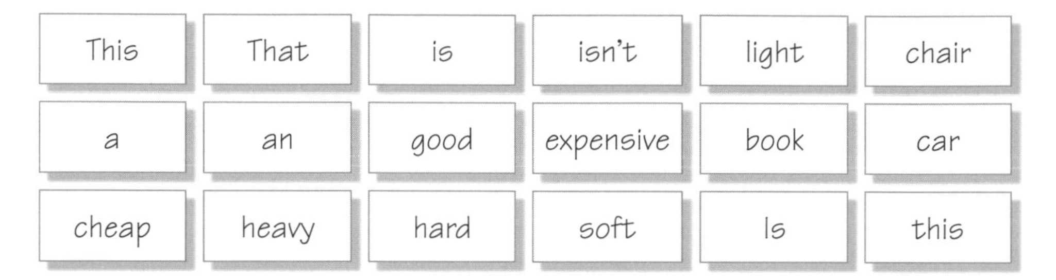


## Colors (Dictionary, p. 12)

### *WH-* QUESTIONS: *WHAT; THIS/THAT, THESE/THOSE*

**Around the Table**
Teacher's Notes, p. 7

*What color is this? It's blue.*

Practice the question-and-answer forms, emphasizing *this/these* for things nearby and *that/those* for things at a distance. Form groups of four students and assign roles A through D in each group. Have students conduct the Q&A drill.

Student A: What color is this?
Student B: It's blue. What color is that?
Student C: It's red. What color are these?
Student D: They're yellow. What color are those?
Student A: They're green. What color . . . ?

## Prepositions (Dictionary, p. 13)

### PREPOSITIONS OF PLACE: *NEXT TO, UNDER, BETWEEN, ON, IN, IN FRONT OF, BELOW*

**Board Race**
Teacher's Notes, p. 6

*It's next to the pink box. It's under the white box.*

Ask the questions below. Have teams check dictionary page 13 and race to write the complete answers on the board.

| Where is the _______ box? | Answers |
|---|---|
| **1.** pink | **1.** It's between the purple box and the brown box. |
| **2.** yellow | **2.** It's next to the red box. |
| **3.** gray | **3.** It's in front of the turquoise box |
| **4.** blue | **4.** It's in the beige box. |
| **5.** white | **5.** It's on the black box. |
| **6.** black | **6.** It's under the white box. |
| **7.** brown | **7.** It's next to the pink box. |
| **8.** orange | **8.** It's below the green box. |

## Numbers and Measurements (Dictionary, pp. 14–15)

### CARDINAL AND ORDINAL NUMBERS

**Mark My Words**
Teacher's Notes, p. 9

*I have three cats. My first cat is two years old. My second cat is very old.*

After teaching cardinals and ordinals on the dictionary page, write the sentences below on the board. Have students work in teams to determine which sentences contain a mistake and which are correct. Then have teams take turns circling the errors and writing the correct sentences.

1. There are tenth cats in my apartment building.
2. I have three cats in my apartment.
3. My first cat is second years old.
4. The two cat is very old.
5. My cats and I live on the one floor of my apartment building.
6. We live in apartment fifteenth.
7. There are six dogs in our apartment building.
8. My third cats don't like dogs.

**Corrections: 1.** ten; **2.** OK; **3.** two; **4.** second; **5.** first; **6.** fifteen; **7.** OK; **8.** three

### SIMPLE PRESENT

**Peer Dictation**
Teacher's Notes, p. 3

*12 inches equal 1 foot. 1 yard equals 3 feet.*

Write the sentences below on the board or on an overhead transparency, and conceal them from the class. Present the clarification strategy: *Did you say...?* Pair students and assign A/B roles. (Have students sit so that the student who is dictating can see the sentences, but the one who is writing cannot.) Student A dictates first, and then Student B. Have partners check each other's work.

**A Sentences**
1. 1,760 yards equal 1 mile.
2. 1 inch equals 2.54 centimeters.
3. 1 yard equals 3 feet.
4. 75% equals 3/4.

**B Sentences**
1. 12 inches equal 1 foot.
2. 1 yard equals .91 meters.
3. 1.6 kilometers equal 1 mile.
4. 1/2 equals 50%.

## Time (Dictionary, pp. 16–17)

### PREPOSITIONS OF TIME: *FROM... TO, AT*

**Sentence Maker**
Teacher's Notes, p. 12

*They go to work at 8:00 a.m. They work from 8:00 a.m. to 5:00 p.m.*

Write the words below on a copy of the Sentence Maker grid (p. 13). Duplicate and cut apart one set of word cards for each group of four to six students. Have each group use their cards to make sentences or questions, while a group recorder writes them on a separate sheet of paper. Instruct students to make and record as many sentences or questions as they can.

| | | | | | |
|---|---|---|---|---|---|
| They | get up | work | study | Do | they |
| go to bed | at | from | to | 10:00 | 11:00 |
| 3:00 | 5:00 | 6:30 | 8:00 | a.m. | p.m. |

## The Calendar (Dictionary, pp. 18–19)

### *WH-* QUESTIONS: *WHEN;* PREPOSITIONS OF TIME: *IN, ON*

**Around the Table**
Teacher's Notes, p. 7

*When's your birthday? When were you born?*

Practice the question-and-answer forms. Form groups of four students and assign roles A through D in each group. Have students conduct the Q&A drills.

**Round 1: *Wh-* Questions**
Student A: When's your birthday?
Student B: In March. When's your birthday?
Student C: In October. When's your birthday?
Student D: In June. When's your birthday?
Student A: In December.

**Round 2: *Wh-* Questions**
Student A: When were you born?
Student B: On March 15, 1985. When were you born?
Etc.

## Money (Dictionary, p. 20)

### *YES/NO* QUESTIONS; SIMPLE PRESENT: *HAVE*

**Back and Forth**
Teacher's Notes, p. 14

*Do you have change for a dollar? I have only 75 cents.*

Put the model conversation on the board. Introduce the situation and role-play the conversation with volunteers. Have students form groups of three and role-play their own version of the conversation.

Martin needs change for a phone call. He asks two different people.
**Martin:** Excuse me, miss. Do you have change for a dollar?
**Woman:** Sorry, I don't. I have only 75 cents.
**Martin:** That's OK. Thanks anyway.
Excuse me, sir. Do you have change for a dollar?
**Man:** Yes, I do. Here you go.
**Martin:** Thanks very much.
**Man:** You're welcome.

## Shopping (Dictionary, p. 21)

### SIMPLE PRESENT VS. PRESENT CONTINUOUS

**TPR Grammar**
Teacher's Notes, p. 4

*He is looking for a new sweater. It looks terrible.*

Command individuals to perform the actions below. While students are performing each action, ask the class the questions to elicit simple present or present continuous statements.

| Teacher Commands | Teacher Questions |
|---|---|
| Look for a new sweater. | What is she/he looking for? |
| Try on a green sweater. | What is she/he doing first? |
| Say, "It looks terrible." | What's wrong with the sweater? |
| Shop for a red sweater. | What is she/he doing now? |
| Read the price tag ($9.99). | How much does it cost? |
| Say, "I love this sweater." | How does she/he feel about the sweater? |
| Buy the sweater. | What is she/he doing with the sweater? |
| Take it home. | What is she/he doing now? |

## Age and Physical Description (Dictionary, p. 22)

### NOUNS: SINGULAR AND PLURAL

*He's a tall man. They're short men.*

**Answers Up**
Teacher's Notes, p. 2

Make each statement below. Have students indicate whether they heard a singular or plural noun by holding up the card labeled "1" (for singular) or "2+" (for plural).

1. He's a tall man.
2. They're short men.
3. They're adults.
4. Look at these babies!
5. She's an attractive woman.
6. I see a six-year-old boy.
7. He's a cute baby.
8. Look at those girls.

## Describing Hair (Dictionary, p. 23)

### SIMPLE PAST VS. SIMPLE PRESENT AND FUTURE: *BE*

*My hair was short. My hair is long. My hair will be curly next year.*

**Interview**
Teacher's Notes, p. 10

Copy the questions (or the alternative questions) below on a copy of the Interview worksheet (p. 11). Follow the directions on the worksheet to have pairs write their own short answers and then their partners' short answers. Have students write follow-up sentences based on the interview answers.

**Interview Questions**

1. What was your hair like when you were a child?
2. What was your hair like ten years ago?
3. What is your hairstyle now?
4. What will your hairstyle be next year?

**Alternative Questions**

1. What was your favorite hairstyle when you were young?
2. What is your favorite hairstyle now?
3. What is your least favorite hairstyle now?
4. What will your hair be like five years from now?

## Family (Dictionary, pp. 24–25)

### POSSESSIVE NOUNS

*She is Tom's aunt. She's Daniel's wife.*

**Board Race**
Teacher's Notes, p. 6

Ask the questions below. Have teams check the dictionary pages and race to write the complete answers on the board.

| Who is/are . . . | Answers |
|---|---|
| **1.** Lily to Tom? | **1.** She's Tom's sister. |
| **2.** Sara to Tito? | **2.** She's Tito's daughter. |
| **3.** Lu to Emily? | **3.** He's Emily's grandfather. |
| **4.** Mario to Ana? | **4.** He's Ana's father-in-law. |
| **5.** Emily to Alex? | **5.** She's Alex's cousin. |
| **6.** Tom to Min? | **6.** He's Min's grandson. |
| **7.** Tito to Eddie? | **7.** He's Eddie's uncle. |
| **8.** Sara and Felix to Alice? | **8.** They're Alice's cousins. |
| **9.** Dan to Lisa? | **9.** He's Lisa's father. |
| **10.** Sue to Lisa? | **10.** She's Lisa's stepmother. |

### POSSESSIVE NOUNS; CONJUNCTIONS

**Class Go-Around**
Teacher's Notes, p. 5

*Lily is Tom's sister, Chang's daughter, and Min's granddaughter.*

Have students look at the dictionary page as you identify all the different family roles that Lily has. Start the chain drill by saying the first sentence below. Have a student repeat what you've said and add another of Lily's roles. Continue the chain with at least five more students, each one repeating what has been said and adding another family role. Do several chains with different people on the page.

**T:** Lily is Tom's sister.
**S1:** Lily is Tom's sister and Chang's daughter.
**S2:** Lily is Tom's sister, Chang's daughter, and Min's granddaughter.

## Daily Routines (Dictionary, pp. 26–27)

### SIMPLE PRESENT

**Interview**
Teacher's Notes, p. 10

*What time do you wake up? I wake up at 6:00 a.m.*

Copy the questions (or the alternative questions) below on a copy of the Interview worksheet (p. 11). Follow the directions on the worksheet to have pairs write their own short answers and then their partners' short answers. Have students write follow-up sentences based on the interview answers.

**Interview Questions**
1. What time do you wake up?
2. What time do you eat breakfast?
3. What time do you go to school?
4. What time do you eat lunch?

**Alternative Questions**
1. Do you make your lunch or buy it?
2. Do you watch TV at night?
3. Do you exercise? When?
4. What time do you go to sleep?

## Life Events (Dictionary, pp. 28–29)

### SIMPLE PAST: STATEMENTS AND QUESTIONS

**Answers Up**
Teacher's Notes, p. 2

*Martin was born in 1925. Where was he born?*

Say each statement or question below. Have students indicate whether they heard a statement or a question by holding up the card labeled "." (for a statement) or "?" (for a question).

1. Martin was born in 1925.
2. Where was he born?
3. He was born in Mexico.
4. He immigrated to the United States in 1940.
5. When did he become a citizen?
6. He became a citizen nine years later.
7. Between 1940 and 1949, he graduated from high school, joined the army, and got a job.
8. Why did Martin like college life?
9. What happened to him in college?
10. He fell in love with his future wife.

## **Feelings** (Dictionary, pp. 30–31)

### *YES/NO* QUESTIONS; ADVERBS OF DEGREE: *NOT AT ALL, A LITTLE, VERY*

**Around the Table**
Teacher's Notes, p. 7

*Are you tired? I'm a little tired. I'm not sad at all.*

Practice the question-and-answer forms. Form groups of four students and assign roles A through D in each group. Have students conduct the Q&A drill.

Student A: Are you bored?
Student B: No, I'm not bored at all. Are you tired?
Student C: Yes, I'm a little tired. Are you hungry?
Student D: Yes, I'm very hungry. Are you . . . ?

### *WH-* QUESTIONS: *WHY*

**Board Race**
Teacher's Notes, p. 6

*Why is he thinking about water? Because he's thirsty.*

Ask the questions below. Have teams check the dictionary pages and race to write the because phrases on the board.

| Why is she/he... /Why are they... | Answers |
|---|---|
| **1.** thinking about water? | **1.** Because he's thirsty. |
| **2.** looking out the window? | **2.** Because he's bored. |
| **3.** sitting alone? | **3.** Because he's lonely. |
| **4.** holding her stomach? | **4.** Because she's in pain. |
| **5.** looking at a photo? | **5.** Because he's homesick. |
| **6.** pointing at her watch? | **6.** Because she's angry. |
| **7.** smiling at each other? | **7.** Because they're in love. |
| **8.** lying on the couch? | **8.** Because they're tired. |
| **9.** hugging her daughter? | **9.** Because she's relieved. |
| **10.** holding his stomach? | **10.** Because he's full. |

## **A Graduation** (Dictionary, pp. 32–33)

### PRESENT CONTINUOUS

**TPR Grammar**
Teacher's Notes, p. 4

*What's he doing? What are they doing?*

Command individuals and groups to perform the actions below. While students are performing each action, ask the class the questions to elicit present continuous statements.

| **Teacher Commands** | **Teacher Questions** |
|---|---|
| Applaud for your classmates. | What's he doing? |
| Laugh at the picture. | What are they doing? |
| Hug your friend. | What are you doing? |
| Dance to the door. | What's she doing? |
| Take a picture of your friend. | What are they doing? |
| Make a toast to your friend. | What are you doing? |
| Give a speech about your friend. | What is he doing? |

## Places to Live, Finding a Home (Dictionary, pp. 34–35)

### PRESENT CONTINUOUS

**Sentence Maker**
Teacher's Notes, p. 12

*They are renting an apartment in the city.*

Write the words below on a copy of the Sentence Maker grid (p. 13). Duplicate and cut apart one set of word cards for each group of four to six students. Have each group use their cards to make sentences or questions, while a group recorder writes them on a separate sheet of paper. Instruct students to make and record as many sentences or questions as they can.

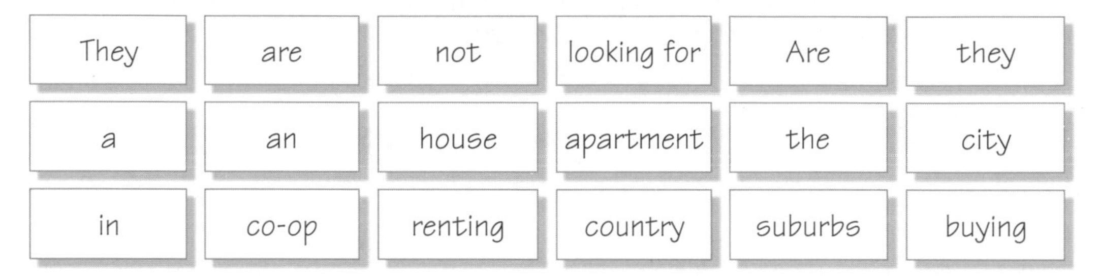


## Apartments (Dictionary, pp. 36–37)

### *YES/NO* QUESTIONS; *THERE IS*

**Back and Forth**
Teacher's Notes, p. 14

*Is there a garage? Yes, there is.*

Put the model conversation on the board. Introduce the situation and role-play the conversation with volunteers. Have students form groups of three and role-play their own version of the conversation.

Two friends are making a phone call to a landlord.
**Friend 1:** Hi, I'm calling about the apartment for rent. We have a car. Is there a garage?
**Landlord:** Yes, there is. There's one parking space for each apartment.
**Friend 2:** Ask about the pool!
**Friend 1:** Is there a swimming pool?
**Landlord:** No, I'm sorry, there isn't. There is a recreation room, though.
**Friend 1:** *(to Friend 2)* There isn't any pool, but there's a rec room. *(to landlord)* Is there a good time to see the apartment?
**Landlord:** You can come by at 2:00 P.M.
**Friend 1:** Great! We'll see you around 2:00 P.M.

## A House (Dictionary, p. 38)

### SIMPLE PRESENT: *NEED*

**Peer Dictation**
Teacher's Notes, p. 3

*It needs a new front door.*

Write the sentences below on the board or on an overhead transparency, and conceal them from the class. Present the clarification strategy: *It needs what...?* Pair students and assign A/B roles. (Have students sit so that the student who is dictating can see the sentences, but the one who is writing cannot.) Student A dictates first, and then Student B. Have partners check each other's work.

**A Sentences**
1. Sara's house needs a lot of work.
2. It needs a new front door.
3. It needs new shutters.
4. The backyard needs a new fence.

**B Sentences**
1. Jim's house needs some work.
2. It needs a new screen door.
3. It needs new gutters.
4. The garage needs a new garage door.

## A Yard (Dictionary, p. 39)

### *NEED* + INFINITIVE VS. *NEED* + NOUN

**Tic-Tac-Toe**
Teacher's Notes, p. 8

*What do you need to plant a tree? You need a shovel.*

Copy the Tic-Tac-Toe grid onto the board or an overhead transparency. Play the game, using the suggested prompts.

| | | |
|---|---|---|
| plant some flowers | water the plants | plant a tree |
| weed the lawn | trim the hedge | rake the leaves |
| mow the lawn | water the lawn | weed the flower bed |

**Round 1**
Prompt: *What do you need to plant a tree?*
Students base their responses on the pictures in the dictionary (e.g., *You need a shovel.*).

**Round 2**
Prompt: *What do you need to do in your yard?*
Students respond with *I need to…*

## A Kitchen (Dictionary, p. 40)

### *WH-* QUESTIONS: *WHERE;* PREPOSITIONS OF PLACE: *ON, ABOVE, NEXT TO*

**Around the Table**
Teacher's Notes, p. 7

*Where's the toaster? It's on the counter.*

Practice the question-and-answer forms. Form groups of four students and assign roles A through D in each group. Have students conduct the Q&A drill, based on the pictures in the dictionary.

Student A: Where's the toaster?
Student B: It's on the counter. Where's the refrigerator?
Student C: It's next to the sink. Where's the microwave?
Student D: It's above the stove. Where's the… ?
Etc.

## A Dining Area (Dictionary, p. 41)

### NOUNS: SINGULAR AND PLURAL; *THERE IS/THERE ARE*

**Class Go-Around**
Teacher's Notes, p. 3

*There are five place mats, and there's one teapot.*

Have students look at the dictionary page as you identify the name and quantity of some of the items in the dining room. Start the chain drill by saying the first sentence below. Have a student repeat what you've said and add another object. Continue the chain with at least five more students, each one repeating what has been said and adding another object.

**T:** There are five place mats in this dining room.
**S1:** There are five place mats, and there's one teapot in this dining room.
**S2:** There are five place mats, there's one teapot, and there are two candlesticks in this dining room.

## A Living Room (Dictionary, p. 42)

### PREPOSITIONS OF PLACE: *IN FRONT OF, NEXT TO, BETWEEN, ON THE RIGHT/LEFT*

**Back and Forth**
Teacher's Notes, p. 14

*Put it in front of the window. Put it next to the sofa, on the left.*

Put the model conversation on the board. Introduce the situation and role-play the conversation with volunteers. Have students form groups of three and role-play their own version of the conversation.

Pat is talking to the movers.
**Mover 1:** Where does this sofa go?
**Pat:** Put it in front of the window.
**Mover 2:** How about this bookcase? Where does it go?
**Pat:** Put it next to the sofa, on the left.
**Mover 2:** Here?
**Pat:** No, next to the wall. The end table goes between the sofa and the bookcase.
**Mover 1:** You want the end table here, right?
**Pat:** Yes. That looks great! Thank you.

## A Bathroom (Dictionary, p. 43)

### PREPOSITIONS OF PLACE: *NEXT TO, IN FRONT OF, ABOVE, UNDER, IN, ON, ACROSS FROM*

**Mark My Words**
Teacher's Notes, p. 9

*The hamper is next to the tub.*

Write the sentences below on the board. Have students look at the dictionary picture to determine which sentences contain a mistake and which are correct. Then have teams take turns circling the errors and writing the correct sentences.

1. The hamper is across from the tub.
2. The mother and child are under the bath mat.
3. The scale is in front of the wastebasket.
4. The blue towels are above the window.
5. The toothbrushes are in the sink.
6. The rubber mat is next to the tub.
7. The medicine cabinet is above the sink.
8. The soap is next to the soap dish.

**Corrections: 1.** next to; **2.** on; **3.** OK; **4.** under; **5.** on; **6.** in; **7.** OK; **8.** on

## A Bedroom (Dictionary, p. 44)

### SIMPLE PAST: *BE;* PREPOSITIONS OF PLACE: *IN, ON, UNDER*

**Sentence Maker**
Teacher's Notes, p. 12

*Was the slipper under the rug? It wasn't on the bed.*

Write the words below on a copy of the Sentence Maker grid (p. 13). Duplicate and cut apart one set of word cards for each group of four to six students. Have each group use their cards to make sentences or questions, while a group recorder writes them on a separate sheet of paper. Instruct students to make and record as many sentences or questions as they can.

| | | | | | |
|---|---|---|---|---|---|
| The | Was | was | wasn't | the | slipper |
| under | in | on | the | drawer | rug |
| bed | night table | closet | dresser | pillow | It |

## A Children's Bedroom (Dictionary, p. 45)

### *THERE IS/THERE ARE*

*There's one doll. There are two beds.*

**Board Race**
Teacher's Notes, p. 6

Ask the questions below. Have teams check the dictionary page and race to write the complete answers on the board.

| How many... are there? | Answers |
|---|---|
| **1.** puzzles | **1.** There is one puzzle. |
| **2.** cribs | **2.** There is one crib. |
| **3.** balls | **3.** There is one ball. |
| **4.** drawers | **4.** There are five drawers. |
| **5.** dolls | **5.** There is one doll. |
| **6.** children | **6.** There are two children. |
| **7.** pillows | **7.** There are two pillows. |

## Housework, Cleaning Supplies (Dictionary, pp. 46–47)

### SIMPLE PRESENT: *USE*

*What do you use to sweep the floor? You use a broom and a dustpan.*

**Tic-Tac-Toe**
Teacher's Notes, p. 8

Copy the Tic-Tac-Toe grid onto the board or an overhead transparency. Play the game, using the suggested prompt.

| | | |
|---|---|---|
| dust the furniture | wash the windows | sweep the floor |
| polish the furniture | clean the oven | mop the floor |
| dry the dishes | wash the dishes | scrub the floor |

**Round 1**
Prompt: *What do you use to... ?*
Students respond with *You use...* , based on the pictures in the dictionary.

**Round 2**
Students on the same team ask and answer the question *What do you use to... ?*

## Household Problems and Repairs (Dictionary, pp. 48–49)

### SIMPLE PRESENT: *NEED;* ADVERBIAL CLAUSES WITH *BECAUSE*

*I need to call a plumber because the faucet is leaking.*

**Peer Dictation**
Teacher's Notes, p. 3

Write the sentences below on the board or on an overhead transparency, and conceal them from the class. Present the clarification strategy: *Because what?* Pair students and assign A/B roles. (Have students sit so that the student who is dictating can see the sentences, but the one who is writing cannot.) Student A dictates first, and then Student B. Have partners check each other's work.

**A Sentences**
1. Susan needs to call a plumber because the pipes are leaking.
2. She needs to call an electrician because the power is out.
3. She needs to call a locksmith because the lock is broken.

**B Sentences**
1. Manuel needs to call a roofer because the roof is leaking.
2. He needs to call a carpenter because the steps are broken.
3. He needs to call a repair person because the furnace isn't working.

## Fruit, Vegetables (Dictionary, pp. 50–51)

### NOUNS: COUNT AND NONCOUNT

**Around the Table**
Teacher's Notes, p. 7

*I need to buy five apples. How much celery do you need? I need two bunches.*

Practice the question-and-answer forms. Form groups of four students and assign roles A through D in each group. Have students conduct the Q&A drills.

**Round 1: Statements**
Student A: I need to buy five apples. How about you?
Student B: I need to buy a head of lettuce. How about you?
Etc.

**Round 2: *Wh-* Questions**
Student A: How many lemons do you need?
Student B: I need one lemon. How much celery do you need?
Student C: I need two bunches of celery. How many sweet peppers do you need?
Student D: I need two sweet peppers.

## Meat and Poultry, Deli and Seafood (Dictionary, pp. 52–53)

### SIMPLE PRESENT; ADVERBS OF FREQUENCY

**Interview**
Teacher's Notes, p. 10

*How often do you eat steak? I never eat steak. I usually eat steak once a week.*

Copy the questions (or the alternative questions) below on a copy of the Interview worksheet (p. 11). Follow the directions on the worksheet to have pairs write their own short answers and then their partners' short answers. Have students write follow-up sentences based on interview answers.

**Interview Questions**
1. How often do you eat steak?
2. How often do you eat bacon?
3. How often do you eat roast beef?
4. How often do you eat cheese?

**Alternative Questions**
1. How often do you eat lobster?
2. How often do you eat shrimp?
3. How often do you eat duck?
4. How often do you eat potato salad?

## The Market (Dictionary, pp. 54–55)

### NOUNS: COUNT AND NONCOUNT; SIMPLE PAST

**Class Go-Around**
Teacher's Notes, p. 5

*I went to the market and bought some eggs. I went to market and bought some eggs and a cake.*

Have students look at the dictionary page as you identify which items in the market are countable (e.g., *a cake, an egg, some eggs*) and which are not (e.g., *some bread, some soup, some flour*). Start the chain drill by saying the first sentence below. Have a student repeat what you've said and add another item from the market. Continue the chain with at least five more students, each one repeating what has been said and adding another food item.

**T:** I went to the market and bought some eggs and a cake.
**S1:** I went to the market and bought some eggs, a cake, and some apple juice.

## Containers and Packaged Foods (Dictionary, p. 56)

### NOUNS: COUNT AND NONCOUNT; SIMPLE PRESENT: THIRD PERSON

**Peer Dictation**
Teacher's Notes, p. 3

*Two cans of soup cost $.69. A jar of jam costs $1.09.*

Write the sentences below on the board or on an overhead transparency, and conceal them from the class. Present the clarification strategies: *How many?* and *How much?* Pair students and assign A/B roles. (Have students sit so that the student who is dictating can see the sentences, but the one who is writing cannot.) Student A dictates first, and then Student B. Have partners check each other's work.

**A Sentences**
1. Two cans of soup cost $.69.
2. Two rolls of paper towels cost $1.50.
3. A jar of jam costs $1.09.
4. Twelve cans of soda cost $2.99.

**B Sentences**
1. A loaf of bread costs $1.39.
2. Four packages of cookies cost $5.00.
3. A bag of flour costs $1.89.
4. Three boxes of cereal cost $3.65.

## Weights and Measures (Dictionary, p. 57)

### NOUNS: COUNT AND NONCOUNT; *HOW MUCH? HOW MANY?*

**Sentence Maker**
Teacher's Notes, p. 12

*How much flour do we need? How many cups of flour do we need?*

Write the words below on a copy of the Sentence Maker grid (p. 13). Duplicate and cut apart one set of word cards for each group of four to six students. Have each group use their cards to make sentences or questions, while a group recorder writes them on a separate sheet of paper. Instruct students to make and record as many sentences or questions as they can.

## Food Preparation (Dictionary, p. 58)

### ADVERBS OF MANNER

**TPR Grammar**
Teacher's Notes, p. 4

*Break the eggs slowly. Beat the eggs well.*

Command individuals and groups to perform the actions below. After students perform each action, ask the class the questions to elicit the adverbs.

**Teacher Commands**
Carefully pick up two eggs.
Break the eggs into the bowl slowly!
Beat the eggs well.
Add sugar to the eggs gracefully.
Quickly mix the flour into the eggs and sugar.
Stir the ingredients happily.

**Teacher Questions**
How did he pick up the eggs?
How did she break the eggs?
How did they beat the eggs?
How did he add the sugar?
How did she mix the flour?
How did he stir the ingredients?

## Kitchen Utensils (Dictionary, p. 59)

### *USE* + INFINITIVE VS. *USE* + NOUN; SIMPLE PRESENT

**Board Race**
Teacher's Notes, p. 6

*What do you use to grate cheese? You use a grater.*

Ask the questions below. Have teams check the dictionary page and race to write the complete answers on the board.

| What do you use to... | Answers |
|---|---|
| **1.** open cans? | **1.** You use a can opener. |
| **2.** grate cheese? | **2.** You use a grater. |
| **3.** steam vegetables? | **3.** You use a steamer. |
| **4.** press garlic? | **4.** You use a garlic press. |
| **5.** time your cooking? | **5.** You use a kitchen timer. |
| **6.** strain spaghetti? | **6.** You use a strainer. |
| **7.** peel carrots? | **7.** You use a vegetable peeler. |
| **8.** beat eggs? | **8.** You use an eggbeater. |

## Fast Food, A Coffee Shop Menu (Dictionary, pp. 60–61)

### FUTURE: *WILL*; NOUNS: COUNT AND NONCOUNT

**Class Go-Around**
Teacher's Notes, p. 5

*I'll have a hamburger with ketchup, an order of french fries, and a salad.*

Have students look at the dictionary pages as you identify which items are countable (e.g., *a muffin, a milk shake, a donut*) and which require additional language to make them countable (e.g., *an order of french fries, a slice of pie, a cup of coffee*). Start the chain drill by saying the first sentence below. Have a student repeat what you've said and order another item. Continue the chain with at least five more students, each one repeating the previous orders and ordering another food item.

**T:** I'll have a hamburger with ketchup.
**S1:** I'll have a hamburger with ketchup and an order of french fries.
**S2:** I'll have a hamburger with ketchup, an order of french fries, and a salad.

## A Restaurant (Dictionary, pp. 62–63)

### PREPOSITIONS OF PLACE: *ON, NEXT TO, ABOVE, ON THE RIGHT/LEFT, TO THE RIGHT/LEFT*

**Peer Dictation**
Teacher's Notes, p. 3

*The napkin goes next to the dinner plate, on the left.*

Write the sentences below on the board or an on overhead transparency, and conceal them from the class. Present the clarification strategy of repeating information with a question intonation: *On the left?* Pair students and assign A/B roles. (Have students sit so that the student who is dictating can see the sentences, but the one who is writing cannot.) Student A dictates first, and then Student B. Have partners check each other's work.

**A Sentences**
1. The napkin goes next to the dinner plate, on the left.
2. The dinner fork goes on the napkin.
3. The salad fork goes to the left of the dinner fork.
4. The soup bowl goes on the plate.

**B Sentences**
1. The knife goes next to the dinner plate, on the right.
2. The spoon goes to the right of the knife.
3. The water glass goes above the plate, to the left.
4. The cup goes above the spoon, to the right.

## Clothing I (Dictionary, pp. 64–65)

### PRESENT CONTINUOUS

*What's he wearing? He's wearing a shirt and jeans.*

**Around the Table**
Teacher's Notes, p. 7

Practice the question-and-answer forms. Form groups of four students and assign roles A through D in each group. Have students conduct the Q&A drills, based on the pictures in the dictionary and their own clothing.

**Round 1: *Wh-* Questions**
Student A: *(pointing to girl in dictionary)* She's wearing a black dress. *(pointing to young man in dictionary)* What's he wearing?
Student B: He's wearing a shirt and jeans. *(pointing to woman in dictionary)* What's she wearing?
Etc.

**Round 2: *Wh-* Questions**
Student A: I'm wearing pants, a shirt, and a sweater. What are you wearing?
Student B: I'm wearing jeans and a T-shirt. What are you wearing?
Etc.

### FUTURE: *GOING TO*

*Are you going to go to the party? I'm going to wear my favorite jeans.*

**Back and Forth**
Teacher's Notes, p. 14

Put the model conversation on the board. Introduce the situation and role-play the conversation with a volunteer. Have students form pairs and role-play their own version of the conversation.

Kim and Jan are discussing their clothing for a party.
**Kim:** Are you going to go to the party on Saturday?
**Jan:** Yes, I am. I'm going to wear my favorite jeans and a sweater.
**Kim:** Well, I'm going to buy a new T-shirt for the party.
**Jan:** Why are you going to do that?
**Kim:** Because a party is a great excuse to buy new clothes.

## Clothing II (Dictionary, p. 66)

### *SHOULD*

*You should wear a jacket. Should I wear a cap? Yes, you should.*

**Tic-Tac-Toe**
Teacher's Notes, p. 8

Copy the Tic-Tac-Toe grid onto the board or an overhead transparency. Play the game, using the suggested prompts.

| windy | raining | sunny |
|---|---|---|
| snowing | hot | cold |
| freezing | icy | cool |

**Round 1**
Prompt: *It's... What should I wear?*
Students respond with *You should wear a...*, based on the picture in the dictionary.

**Round 2**
Prompt: *Should I wear... ?*
Students respond with *Yes, you should* OR *No, you shouldn't.*

## Clothing III (Dictionary, p. 67)

### QUANTITY EXPRESSIONS: *A* VS. *A PAIR OF*

*The man is wearing a pair of bike shorts.*

**Mark My Words**
Teacher's Notes, p. 9

Write the sentences below on the board. Have students look at the dictionary picture to determine which sentences contain a mistake and which are correct. Then have teams take turns circling the errors and writing the correct sentences.

1. The man on the left is wearing a bike shorts.
2. The woman on the left is wearing a pair of leotard.
3. The girl on the right is wearing a pair of pajamas.
4. The woman on the right is wearing nightgown.
5. The woman on the right is wearing a slippers.
6. The man on the right is wearing a blue bathrobe.
7. The little boy on the right is wearing blanket sleeper.

**Corrections: 1.** pair of; **2.** a leotard; **3.** OK; **4.** a; **5.** pair of; **6.** OK; **7.** a

## Shoes and Accessories (Dictionary, pp. 68–69)

### PRESENT CONTINUOUS: STATEMENTS

*She's looking at a purse. He's trying on shoes.*

**Board Race**
Teacher's Notes, p. 6

Ask the questions below. Have teams check the dictionary page and race to write the complete answers on the board.

| What is the... | Answers |
|---|---|
| **1.** woman in the green sweater doing? | **1.** She's looking at a purse. |
| **2.** woman in the yellow sweater doing? | **2.** She's trying on a silk scarf. |
| **3.** woman in the purple sweater doing? | **3.** She's showing a watch. |
| **4.** woman in the pink suit doing? | **4.** She's looking at the watch. |
| **5.** man in the suspenders doing? | **5.** He's waiting in line. |
| **6.** man in blue jeans doing? | **6.** He's trying on shoes. |

## Describing Clothes (Dictionary, pp. 70–71)

### COMPARATIVES; ADVERBS OF DEGREE: *TOO*

*It's too loose. I need a smaller size.*

**Back and Forth**
Teacher's Notes, p. 14

Put the model conversation on the board. Introduce the situation and role-play the conversation with a volunteer. Have students form pairs and role-play their own version of the conversation.

A customer is shopping for a new sweater.
**Customer:** I'm looking for a yellow sweater.
**Salesperson:** Here, try on this sweater.
**Customer:** It's too loose. I need a smaller size.
**Salesperson:** Okay, try this one.
**Customer:** This one is just right! How much is it?
**Salesperson:** It's $150.00.
**Customer:** Oh, that's too expensive. I need a cheaper one.
**Salesperson:** Here's a medium yellow sweater. It's $19.99.
**Customer:** That's perfect!

## ADJECTIVE ORDER

**Sentence Maker**
Teacher's Notes, p. 12

*I'm looking for a long-sleeved, striped, cotton shirt. I'm looking for blue wool pants.*

Write the words below on a copy of the Sentence Maker grid (p. 13). Duplicate and cut apart one set of word cards for each group of four to six students. Have each group use their cards to make sentences or questions, while a group recorder writes them on a separate sheet of paper. Instruct students to make and record as many sentences or questions as they can.

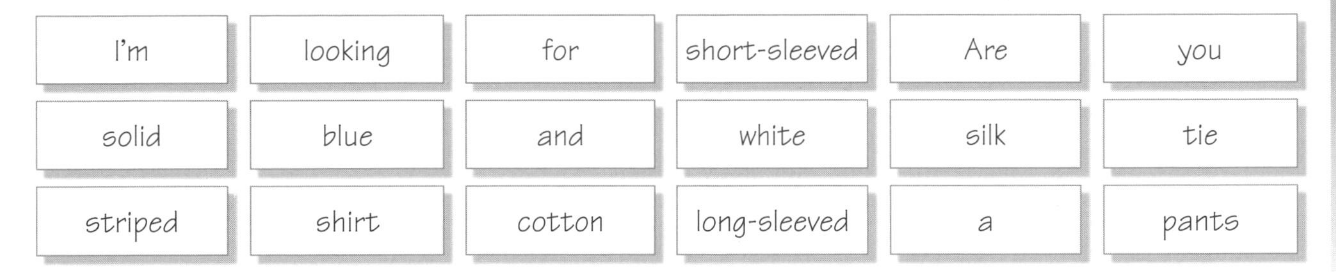


# Doing the Laundry (Dictionary, p. 72)

## SIMPLE PAST: REGULAR AND IRREGULAR FORMS

**TPR Grammar**
Teacher's Notes, p. 4

*What did he do first? First he ironed a shirt. Then he put it on.*

Command individuals and groups to perform the actions below. After students perform each action, ask the class the questions to elicit simple past statements.

| **Teacher Commands** | **Teacher Questions** |
|---|---|
| Sort the laundry. | What did he do? |
| Add the detergent and load the laundry. | What did she do first? What did she do after that? |
| Close the washer. | What did he do? |
| Start the washer. | What did they do? |
| Clean the lint trap. | What did she do? |
| Unload the washer and put the clothes in the dryer. | What did she do first? What did she do after that? |
| Unload the dryer and fold the laundry. | What did they do? |
| Iron a wrinkled shirt and put it on. | What did he do first? What did he do after that? |

# Sewing and Alterations (Dictionary, p. 73)

## ADVERBS OF DEGREE: *TOO;* OBJECT PRONOUNS: *IT, THEM*

**Peer Dictation**
Teacher's Notes, p. 3

*If your suit is too baggy, take it in.*

Write the sentences below on the board or on an overhead transparency, and conceal them from the class. Present the clarification strategy: *How do you spell... ?* Pair students and assign A/B roles. (Have students sit so that the student who is dictating can see the sentences, but the one who is writing cannot.) Student A dictates first, and then Student B. Have partners check each other's work.

**A Sentences**
1. If your pants are too short, lengthen them.
2. If your dress is too tight, let it out.
3. If your sleeves are too narrow, let them out.
4. If your waistband is too loose, take it in.

**B Sentences**
1. If your pants are too long, shorten them.
2. If your sleeves are too wide, take them in.
3. If your suit is too baggy, take it in.
4. If your hemline is too short, lengthen it.

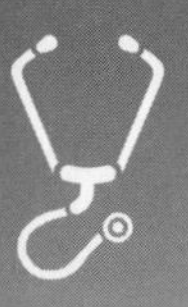

## The Body (Dictionary, pp. 74–75)

### NOUNS: SINGULAR AND PLURAL

**Answers Up**
Teacher's Notes, p. 2

*Put your feet together on the floor. Raise your right knee.*

Give each exercise command below. Have students indicate whether they heard the singular or plural form of the noun by holding up the card labeled "1" (for singular) or "2+" (for plural).

**1.** Put your feet together on the floor.
**2.** Raise your arms up.
**3.** Raise your right knee.
**4.** Put your right foot down.
**5.** Lower your left arm.
**6.** Breathe in and out through your nose.
**7.** Roll your shoulders forward and backward.
**8.** Bend over and touch the floor with your fingers.

## Personal Hygiene (Dictionary, pp. 76–77)

### SIMPLE PRESENT: THIRD PERSON

**Mark My Words**
Teacher's Notes, p. 9

*Magda takes a shower every day.*

Write the sentences below on the board. Have students determine which sentences contain a mistake and which are correct. Then have teams take turns circling the errors and writing the correct sentences.

**1.** Magda take a shower every day.
**2.** She always washs her hair.
**3.** After that, she put sunscreen on her face and neck.
**4.** She likes to uses mouthwash.
**5.** Sometimes she dries her hair with a blow dryer.
**6.** She never use hairspray.
**7.** She doesn't wears perfume or cologne.
**8.** She usually combs her hair before she leaves the house.

**Corrections: 1.** takes; **2.** washes; **3.** puts; **4.** use; **5.** OK; **6.** uses; **7.** wear; **8.** OK

## Symptoms and Injuries, Illnesses and Medical Conditions (Dictionary, pp. 78, 79)

### SIMPLE PRESENT: QUESTIONS AND ANSWERS

**Tic-Tac-Toe**
Teacher's Notes, p. 8

*What's the matter with Tom? He has an ear infection.*

Copy the Tic-Tac-Toe grid onto the board or an overhead transparency. Play the game, using the suggested prompt.

| | | |
|---|---|---|
| headache | toothache | ear infection |
| stomachache | backache | strep throat |
| rash | sunburn | cold |

Prompt: *What's the matter with Tom?*
Students respond with *He has a (an)...*, based on the square.

## Health Care (Dictionary, pp. 80–81)

### SIMPLE PRESENT: TIME EXPRESSIONS

*Tom takes prescription medicine every day.*

**Peer Dictation**
Teacher's Notes, p. 3

Write the sentences below on the board or an overhead transparency, and conceal them from the class. Present the clarification strategy: *How often?* Pair students and assign A/B roles. (Have students sit so that the student who is dictating can see the sentences, but the student who is writing cannot.) Student A dictates first, and then Student B. Have partners check each other's work.

**A Sentences**

1. Tom takes prescription medicine every day.
2. He goes to the pharmacy every two weeks.
3. He goes to a chiropractor once a month.
4. He gets acupuncture treatments now and then.

**B Sentences**

1. Lana wears contact lenses most of the time.
2. She wears glasses now and then.
3. She uses eyedrops once a day.
4. She sees her optometrist twice a year.

## Medical Emergencies, First Aid (Dictionary, pp. 82–83)

### SIMPLE PAST: REGULAR AND IRREGULAR FORMS

*What happened to George? He had a heart attack. He fell down.*

**Back and Forth**
Teacher's Notes, p. 14

Put the model conversation on the board. Introduce the situation and role-play the conversation with a volunteer. Have students form pairs and role-play their own version of the conversation.

Two neighbors are discussing another neighbor's emergency.
**Neighbor 1:** I'm going to visit George in the hospital. Do you want to come?
**Neighbor 2:** What happened to him?
**Neighbor 1:** He had a heart attack, so his wife called 911.
**Neighbor 2:** Oh, no! Is he OK?
**Neighbor 1:** Well, yesterday he fell in the hospital and broke his leg.
**Neighbor 2:** Oh, no! That's terrible.
**Neighbor 1:** He's doing much better now.
**Neighbor 2:** Great. Let's go visit him.

## Clinics (Dictionary, p. 84)

### *HAVE TO* FOR NECESSITY

*He has to see the receptionist. You don't have to see the doctor.*

**Sentence Maker**
Teacher's Notes, p. 12

Write the words below on a copy of the Sentence Maker grid (p. 13). Duplicate and cut apart one set of word cards for each group of four to six students. Have each group use their cards to make sentences or questions, while a group recorder writes them on a separate sheet of paper. Instruct students to make and record as many sentences or questions as they can.

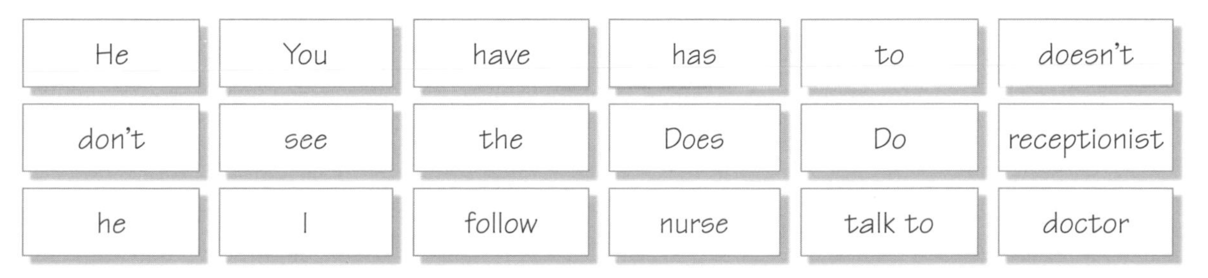

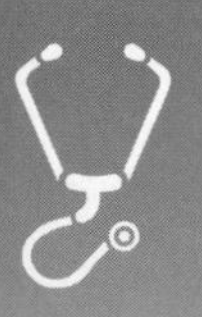

## Medical and Dental Exams (Dictionary, p. 85)

### SIMPLE PRESENT

*Does the doctor check your air pressure or your blood pressure? What does a dentist do?*

**Tic-Tac-Toe**
Teacher's Notes, p. 8

Copy the Tic-Tac-Toe grid onto the board or an overhead transparency. Play the game, using the suggested prompts.

| check | take | listen to |
|---|---|---|
| look in | draw | examine |
| clean | drill | fill |

**Round 1**
Prompt: *Does the doctor check your air pressure or your blood pressure?*
Students respond with complete sentences based on the dictionary page.

**Round 2**
Prompt: *What does a dentist do?*
Students respond with complete sentences based on the dictionary page (e.g., *A dentist drills your teeth.*).

## A Hospital (Dictionary, pp. 86–87)

### OBJECT PRONOUNS: *HIM, HER, THEM*

*I need to talk to the obstetrician. I need to talk to her.*

**Answers Up**
Teacher's Notes, p. 2

State each set of complete and incomplete sentences below. Have students look in their dictionaries and complete each incomplete sentence by holding up the object pronoun card labeled "HIM," "HER," or "THEM."

1. I need to talk to the obstetrician. I need to talk to ________.
2. I have to find the EMTs. I have to find ________.
3. I want to speak with the lab technician. I want to speak with ________
4. I have to see my internist. I have to see ________.
5. I need to find the dietician. I have to find ________.
6. I have to call the RN. I have to call ________.
7. I need to contact the surgeon. I need to contact ________.
8. I want to discuss something with the nurses. I want to discuss something with ________.

**Answers: 1.** her; **2.** them; **3.** him; **4.** him; **5.** her; **6.** her; **7.** him; **8.** them

### SUBJECT AND OBJECT PRONOUNS; SIMPLE PRESENT

*Where do nurses put the medications? They put them on a medication tray.*

**Board Race**
Teacher's Notes, p. 6

Ask the questions below. Have teams check the dictionary page and race to write the complete answers on the board.

| Questions | Answers |
|---|---|
| **1.** Where do nurses put the medications? | **1.** They put them on a medication tray. |
| **2.** Where does the patient sleep? | **2.** He sleeps in a hospital bed. |
| **3.** Where do internists write medical information? | **3.** They write it on medical charts. |
| **4.** What do surgeons wear on their heads? | **4.** They wear surgical caps. |
| **5.**What does the patient use to call the nurse? | **5.** He uses a call button. |
| **6.** Where do nurses read patients' vital signs? | **6.** They read them on a vital signs monitor. |
| **7.** Where do the EMTs put the patient? | **7.** They put him on a gurney. |

## City Streets (Dictionary, pp. 88–89)

### IMPERATIVES; PREPOSITIONS OF PLACE: *AT, ON, ON/TO THE CORNER OF*

**TPR Grammar**
Teacher's Notes, p. 4

*Stand on the corner of Elm and Main. Walk one block east and turn left. He's on Pine.*

Identify the aisles of the classroom as streets in the picture in the dictionary. Identify "blocks" on the streets. Command groups and individuals to perform the actions below. After students perform each action, ask the class the questions about the students' location.

| Teacher Commands | Teacher Questions |
|---|---|
| Stand on the corner of Elm and Main. | Is he at the coffee shop or the bakery? |
| Walk one block east and turn left. | Is he on Pine or Main? |
| Walk two blocks and turn right. | Is he at the market or the car dealership? |
| Stand on the corner of Main and Oak. | Is she at the health club or the police station? |
| Walk north on Oak, one block to the school. | Is she on Oak or Main? |
| Make a left on First and walk two blocks to the corner of First and Elm. | Is she at the movie theater or the car dealership? |
| Start at the bank. | Are they on Elm or Main Street. |
| Walk south to Main Street and cross the street. | Where are they? |

## An Intersection (Dictionary, pp. 90–91)

### *CAN* FOR POSSIBILITY; QUANTIFIERS: *ONE, SOME*

**Board Race**
Teacher's Notes, p. 6

*Where can I buy a newspaper? You can buy one at the newsstand.*

Ask the questions below. Have teams check the dictionary page and race to write the complete answers on the board.

| Where can I... | Answers |
|---|---|
| **1.** buy a newspaper? | **1.** You can buy one at the newsstand. |
| **2.** get some donuts? | **2.** You can get some at the donut shop. |
| **3.** make some copies? | **3.** You can make some at the copy center. |
| **4.** buy a bottle of water? | **4.** You can buy one at the convenience store. |
| **5.** get a hamburger? | **5.** You can get one at the fast-food restaurant. |
| **6** buy some aspirin? | **6.** You can buy some at the drugstore. |
| **7.** buy an ice-cream cone? | **7.** You can buy one in the park. |
| **8.** buy some film for my camera? | **8.** You can buy some at the photo shop. |

### *THERE IS... /IS THERE... ?*

**Around the Table**
Teacher's Notes, p. 7

*There's a nail salon in this part of town. Is there a newsstand near here?*

Practice the question-and-answer forms. Form groups of four students and assign roles A through D in each group. Have students conduct the Q&A drills.

**Round 1: Statements**
Student A: There's a nail salon in this part of town. What else is there?
Student B: There's a photo shop in this part of town. What else is there?
Etc.

**Round 2: Yes/No Questions**
Student A: Is there a newsstand near here?
Student B: Yes, there is. It's near the Burger Queen. Is there a dry cleaners near here?
Student C: Yes, there is. It's near the nail salon. Is there a donut shop near here?
Student D: Yes, there is. It's near the copy center. Is there a... near here?

## A Mall (Dictionary, pp. 92–93)

### ADVERBIAL CLAUSES WITH *BECAUSE*

**Class Go-Around**
Teacher's Notes, p. 5

*I'm going to the card store because I need a birthday card.*

Have students look at the dictionary page. Elicit items to buy and things to do at each of the mall stores. Start the chain drill by saying the first sentence below. Have a student repeat what you've said and add another store and another item. Continue the chain with at least five more students, each one repeating what has been said and adding another store and another item.

**T:** I'm going to the card store because I need a birthday card.
**S1:** I'm going to the card store because I need a birthday card. Then I'm going to the bookstore because I need a new book.

## A Childcare Center (Dictionary, pp. 94–95)

### COMPARATIVES

**Peer Dictation**
Teacher's Notes, p. 3

*A rattle is noisier than a pacifier. A pacifier is quieter than a rattle.*

Write the sentences below on the board or on an overhead transparency, and conceal them from the class. Present the clarification strategy: *Could you repeat the first/last part?* Pair students and assign A/B roles. (Have students sit so that the student who is dictating can see the sentences, but the one who is writing cannot.) Student A dictates first, and then Student B. Have partners check each other's work.

**A Sentences**
1. A rattle is noisier than a pacifier.
2. A stroller is cheaper than a carriage.
3. It's easier to change diapers on a changing table than on a bed.
4. Car safety seats are safer in the back seat than in the front seat.

**B Sentences**
1. A pacifier is quieter than a rattle.
2. A carriage is more expensive than a stroller.
3. It's more difficult to change diapers on a bed than on a changing table.
4. Car safety seats are less safe in the front seat than in the back seat.

## U.S. Mail (Dictionary, p. 96)

### SIMPLE PRESENT VS. SIMPLE PAST

**TPR Grammar**
Teacher's Notes, p. 4

*You fold the letter. They folded the letter.*

Using props, first ask the class Question #1 below to elicit simple present statements. Then command two or more students to perform each action. After students perform each action, ask the class Question #2 to elicit simple past statements.

| Question #1 | Commands | Question #2 |
|---|---|---|
| What do you fold? | Fold your letter. | What did they fold? |
| What do you do with the letter? | Put the letter in an envelope. | Where did they put it? |
| What do you do next? | Address the envelope. | What did they address? |
| What do you write in the upper left corner? | Write the return address. | Where did they write it? |
| What do you put on the envelope? | Put a stamp on the envelope. | Where did they walk? |
| Where do you walk? | Walk to the mailbox. | Where did they put it? |
| What do you do with the letter? | Mail the letter. | What did they do with the letter? |

## A Bank (Dictionary, p. 97)

### SIMPLE PRESENT VS. PRESENT CONTINUOUS

*She's inserting her ATM card. The machine always asks you to insert your card.*

**Answers Up**
Teacher's Notes, p. 2

Have students look at pictures A–F on dictionary page 97. Make each statement below. Have students hold up the card labeled "NOW" when they hear about something that is currently happening (the present continuous) or the card labeled "REGULARLY" when they heard about something that occurs regularly (the simple present).

1. She's inserting her ATM card.
2. The machine always asks you to insert your card.
3. You usually enter your PIN number.
4. She's entering her PIN number.
5. Before you can make a deposit, you have to fill out a deposit slip.
6. She's making a deposit of $150.00 at the ATM.
7. She's also withdrawing $40.00 in cash.
8. Usually the ATM gives you only twenty-dollar bills.

## A Library (Dictionary, p. 98)

### *WH-* QUESTIONS: *WHICH;* SIMPLE PRESENT

*Which do you read more often, newspapers or magazines? I read magazines more often.*

**Interview**
Teacher's Notes, p. 10

Copy the questions (or the alternative questions) below on a copy of the Interview worksheet (p. 11). Follow the directions on the worksheet to have pairs write their own short answers and then their partners' short answers. Have students write follow-up sentences based on interview answers.

**Interview Questions**
1. Which do you read more often, newspapers or magazines?
2. Which do you listen to more often, CDs or audiocassettes?
3. Which do you think is more interesting, an atlas or an encyclopedia?
4. Which do you like more, fiction books or nonfiction books?

**Alternative Questions**
1. Which do you prefer to do, check books out of the library or buy them?
2. Which do you do more often, read or watch videocassettes?
3. Which do use more often, the online catalog or the card catalog?
4. Which do you think most people use more, their ATM cards or their library cards?

## The Legal System (Dictionary, p. 99)

### SIMPLE PAST

*What did the police do? They arrested the suspect. Who arrested the suspect? The police did.*

**Tic-Tac-Toe**
Teacher's Notes, p. 8

Copy the Tic-Tac-Toe grid onto the board or an overhead transparency. Play the game, using the suggested prompts.

| have | arrest | hire |
|---|---|---|
| appear | stand | give |
| sentence | go | be |

**Round 1**
Prompt: Who *had the right to remain silent*? [action in past]?
Students respond with *The suspect did*, based on the dictionary page.

**Round 2**
Prompt: What did the suspect do?
Students respond with He/They + simple past, based on the dictionary page.

## Crime (Dictionary, p. 100)

### SIMPLE PAST

**Sentence Maker**
Teacher's Notes, p. 12

*The police arrested Pat for vandalism. Did Pat commit a burglary?*

Write the words below on a copy of the Sentence Maker grid (p. 13). Duplicate and cut apart one set of word cards for each group of four to six students. Have each group use their cards to make sentences or questions, while a group recorder writes them on a separate sheet of paper. Instruct students to make and record as many sentences or questions as they can.

| | | | | | |
|---|---|---|---|---|---|
| The | police | arrested | committed | Pat | drunk driving |
| them | crime | vandalism | for | mugging | gang violence |
| a | Did | murder | burglary | commit | assault |

## Public Safety (Dictionary, p. 101)

### *SHOULD*

**Mark My Words**
Teacher's Notes, p. 9

*You should walk with a friend after dark.*

Write the sentences below on the board. Have students look at the dictionary picture to determine which sentences contain a mistake and which are correct. Then have teams take turns circling the errors and writing the correct sentences.

**1.** You shouldn't walk with a friend after dark.
**2.** You should stay on dark streets.
**3.** Women should hold their purses far from their bodies.
**4.** The police should protect your wallet.
**5.** People should never drink.
**6.** You shouldn't open your door at night.
**7.** You should lock your doors.

**Corrections: 1.** should; **2.** well-lit; **3.** close to; **4.** You; **5.** and drive; **6.** to strangers; **7.** OK;

## Emergencies and Natural Disasters (Dictionary, pp. 102–103)

### PRESENT PERFECT; *TOO, EITHER*

**Around the Table**
Teacher's Notes, p. 7

*Have you ever been in an earthquake? I've never been in a blizzard either.*

Practice the question-and-answer forms. Form groups of four students and assign roles A through D in each group. Have students conduct the Q&A drills.

**Round 1:** ***Yes/No*** **Questions**
Student A: Have you ever experienced a major disaster?
Student B: Yes, I have. I saw a tornado once. Have you ever been in a major disaster?
Etc.

**Round 2: Statements**
Student A: I've never been in an earthquake, but I've been in a hurricane.
Student B: I've been in a hurricane too, but I've never been in a blizzard.
Student C: I've never been in a blizzard either, but I've had a car accident.
Etc.

## Public Transportation (Dictionary, p. 104)

### SIMPLE PRESENT: THIRD-PERSON SINGULAR AND PLURAL

**Answers Up**
Teacher's Notes, p. 2

*They take the bus downtown together. Then Sara takes the subway to work.*

Make each statement below. Have students hold up the card labeled "VERB" to indicate that they heard the third-person plural form of the verb or the card labeled "VERB + *-S/-ES*" to indicate that they heard a third-person singular form.

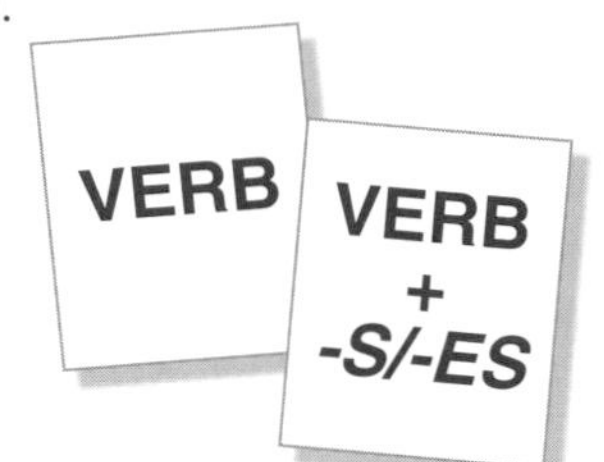


1. George waits at the bus stop every morning with his wife, Sara.
2. They take the bus downtown together.
3. Then Sara takes the subway to work.
4. George works at the subway station information booth.
5. The passengers ask a lot of questions about schedules and fares.
6. At the end of the day, Sara and George walk to the bus station.
7. Sometimes their friend, Singh, picks them up on their way to the bus st
8. On weekends, Sara and George take the ferry to visit friends.

## Prepositions of Motion (Dictionary, p. 105)

### PREPOSITIONS OF MOTION WITH *GET* AND *GO*; ADVERBS OF SEQUENCE

**Class Go-Around**
Teacher's Notes, p. 5

*First she got into a taxi. Then she went through the tunnel.*

Have students look at the dictionary page as you identify whether *get* or *go* is used with the various prepositions of motion (e.g., *get out of a taxi, go over a bridge*). Set the scene by identifying the woman in picture 4 as a police officer and the man in picture 5 as the criminal she is chasing. Start the chain drill by saying the first sentence below. Have a student repeat what you've said and add another step to the chase. Continue the chain with at least five more students, each one repeating what has been said and adding another step.

**T:** The police officer chased the criminal all over town. First she got into a taxi.
**S1:** First she got into a taxi. Then she went through the tunnel.
**S2:** First she got into a taxi. Then she went through the tunnel. Next she …

## Cars and Trucks (Dictionary, p. 106)

### *WH-* QUESTIONS: *WHOSE, HOW MUCH, WHICH*

**Back and Forth**
Teacher's Notes, p. 14

*What kind of car are you looking for?*

Put the model conversation on the board. Introduce the situation and role-play the conversation with a volunteer. Have students form pairs and role-play their own version of the conversation.

A salesperson and a customer at a car dealership are discussing cars.
**Customer:** Hi! I'm looking for a convertible.
**Salesperson:** That yellow convertible was John Wayne's car.
**Customer:** Whose car?
**Salesperson:** John Wayne's. You know, the movie star. It's only $26,000.
**Customer:** How much?!
**Salesperson:** Twenty-six grand. That sports car is only $19,000.
**Customer:** Which sports car?
**Salesperson:** The red one. Hey, where are you going?
**Customer:** To a bike store!

## Directions and Traffic Signs (Dictionary, p. 107)

### *HAVE TO* FOR NECESSITY VS. *CAN* FOR POSSIBILITY

**Board Race**
Teacher's Notes, p. 6

*You have to stop. You can make a U-turn.*

Ask the questions below. Have teams race to write the complete answers on the board.

| Questions | Answers |
|---|---|
| **1.** What do you have to do at a Stop sign? | **1.** You have to stop. |
| **2.** What can you do when you see a U-turn OK sign? | **2.** You can make a U-turn. |
| **3.** What do you have to do when you see a Speed Limit sign? | **3.** You have to drive at the speed limit. |
| **4.** What do you have to do when you see a Pedestrian Crossing sign? | **4.** You have to look for pedestrians. |
| **5.** What do you have to watch for at a railroad crossing? | **5.** You have to watch for trains. |
| **6.** What do you have to do at a school crossing? | **6.** You have to watch for children. |
| **7.** Do you have to turn right when you're in the Right Turn Only lane? | **7.** Yes, you do. |
| **8.** Can you usually turn left from the right lane? | **8.** No, you can't. |

## Parts of a Car and Car Maintenance (Dictionary, pp. 108–109)

### SIMPLE PRESENT: *NEED; YES/NO* QUESTIONS

**Sentence Maker**
Teacher's Notes, p. 12

*The car needs oil. Does it need a new radio?*

Write the words below on a copy of the Sentence Maker Grid (p. 13). Duplicate and cut apart one set of word cards for each group of four to six students. Have each group use their cards to make sentences or questions, while a group recorder writes them on a separate sheet of paper. Instruct students to make and record as many sentences or questions as they can.

## An Airport, A Plane Trip (Dictionary, pp. 110–111)

### SIMPLE PAST; *WH-* QUESTIONS: *WHAT, WHERE, WHO*

**TPR Grammar**
Teacher's Notes, p. 4

*What did he do? He checked his bags.*

Command individuals and groups to perform the actions below. After students perform each action, ask the class the questions to elicit simple past statements.

| **Teacher Commands** | **Teacher Questions** |
|---|---|
| Check your bags at the check-in counter. | What did he do? |
| Go through security. | What did they do? |
| Get your boarding passes from the airline representative. | What did they do? |
| Find your seat. | What did she do? |
| Stow your bag in the overhead compartment. | Where did she put her bag? |
| Fasten your seat belt and put up your tray table. | What did he do? |
| Request a blanket from the flight attendant. | Who did he ask? |
| Get off the plane and go to the baggage claim area. | What did they do? |
| Take your baggage off the carousel. | What did he do? |

## Types of Schools (Dictionary, p. 112)

### SIMPLE PAST; PREPOSITIONS OF TIME: *FROM... TO, FOR*

Peer Dictation
Teacher's Notes, p. 3

*He went to elementary school from 1992 to 1997.*

Write the sentences below on the board or on an overhead transparency, and conceal them from the class. Present the clarification strategies: *When?* and *How long?* Pair students and assign A/B roles. (Have students sit so that the student who is dictating can see the sentences, but the one who is writing cannot.) Student A dictates first, and then Student B. Have partners check each other's work.

**A Sentences**

1. Jack started preschool at age three.
2. He went to elementary school from 1992 to 1997.
3. After that, he went to middle school for three years.
4. In 2004, he graduated from high school.

**B Sentences**

1. Ms Yee went to the adult school for two years.
2. She studied computer technology at a vocational school from 1998 to 1999.
3. After that, she went to a community college for two years.
4. In 2004, she graduated from the state university.

## English Composition (Dictionary, p. 113)

### PUNCTUATION

**Mark My Words**
Teacher's Notes, p. 9

*Do you like to write papers? Don't forget to turn in your papers on time!*

Write the sentences below on the board. Have students determine which sentences contain mistakes and which are correct, according to the dictionary. Then have teams take turns circling the errors and writing the correct sentences.

1. Do you like to write papers
2. there are two things good writers do edit and rewrite
3. Good writers also write drafts get feedback and write a second draft
4. Dont forget to turn in your papers on time
5. you cant get a good grade on a very late paper
6. Start every sentence with a capital letter.

**Corrections. 1.** papers? **2.** There /do:/rewrite. **3.** drafts,/feedback,/draft. **4.** Don't/time! **5.** You/can't/paper. **6.** OK

## U.S. History (Dictionary, pp. 114–115)

### SIMPLE PAST; PREPOSITIONS OF TIME: *IN*

**Board Race**
Teacher's Notes, p. 6

*When did the Civil War start? It started in 1861.*

Ask the questions below. Have teams check the dictionary page and race to write the complete answers on the board.

| Questions | Answers |
|---|---|
| **1.** When did Edison invent the lightbulb? | **1.** He invented it in 1879. |
| **2.** When did Bell invent the telephone? | **2.** He invented it in 1876. |
| **3.** When did Neil Armstrong walk on the moon? | **3.** He walked on the moon in 1969. |
| **4.** When did the civil rights movement start? | **4.** It started in 1954. |
| **5.** When did the Revolutionary War start? | **5.** It started in 1775. |
| **6.** When did the Civil War start? | **6.** It started in 1861. |
| **7.** When did World War II end? | **7.** It ended in 1945. |

## SIMPLE PAST; *YES/NO* QUESTIONS

**Tic-Tac-Toe**
Teacher's Notes, p. 8

*What happened in 1776? Did the Revolutionary War start in 1776?*

Copy the Tic-Tac-Toe grid onto the board or an overhead transparency. Play the game, using the suggested prompts.

| | | |
|---|---|---|
| 1812 | 1776 | 1848 |
| 1861 | 1876 | 1879 |
| 1920 | 1929 | 1969 |

**Round 1**
Prompt: *Did [event in past] in 1776?* (e.g., *Did the Civil War start in 1776?*)
Students respond with *Yes,... did* OR *No,... didn't.*

**Round 2**
Students on the same team ask and answer the question *What happened in... ?*

# U.S. Government and Citizenship (Dictionary, p. 116)

## *MUST* FOR OBLIGATION VS. *SHOULD* FOR ADVISABILITY

**Answers Up**
Teacher's Notes, p. 2

*All citizens must obey the law. All citizens should vote.*

Make each statement below. Have students indicate what they heard by holding up the card labeled "SHOULD" or the card labeled "MUST."

1. Immigrants must be 18 years old to become citizens.
2. They must also take a citizenship test.
3. All citizens should vote.
4. The president of the United States must be 35 years old.
5. You should write to your senator or congressperson.
6. All citizens must obey the law.
7. All males 18 to 26 years old must register with Selective Service.
8. Everyone should serve on a jury at least once.

SHOULD

MUST

# Geography (Dictionary, p. 117)

## *WOULD* AND *WOULDN'T* FOR PREFERENCE

**Sentence Maker**
Teacher's Notes, p. 12

*I'd like to live near an ocean. I wouldn't want to live in the mountains.*

Write the words below on a copy of the Sentence Maker grid (p. 13). Duplicate and cut apart one set of word cards for each group of four to six students. Have each group use their cards to make sentences or questions, while a group recorder writes them on a separate sheet of paper. Instruct students to make and record as many sentences or questions as they can.

| | | | | | |
|---|---|---|---|---|---|
| I | He | 'd | wouldn't | Would | he |
| like | to live | on | in | island | mountains |
| near | an | the | ocean | forest | desert |

## Mathematics (Dictionary, p. 118)

### SIMPLE PRESENT: *HAVE,* THIRD PERSON

*A cube has six sides. A circle has a circumference.*

**Peer Dictation**
Teacher's Notes, p. 3

Write the sentences below on the board or on an overhead transparency, and conceal them from the class. Present the clarification strategy: *It has what?* Pair students and assign A/B roles. (Have students sit so that the student who is dictating can see the sentences, but the one who is writing cannot.) Student A dictates first, and then Student B. Have partners check each other's work.

**A Sentences**
1. A rectangle has four sides.
2. A triangle has three sides.
3. A square has four sides.
4. A circle has a circumference.

**B Sentences**
1. A cube has six sides.
2. A pyramid has five sides.
3. A right triangle has a 90° angle.
4. A cone has a circle at its base.

## Science (Dictionary, p. 119)

### PRESENT CONTINUOUS; *WH-* QUESTIONS: *WHAT, WHY*

*What are you doing? Why are you doing that?*

**Back and Forth**
Teacher's Notes, p. 14

Put the model conversation on the board. Introduce the situation and role-play the conversation with a volunteer. Have students form pairs and role-play their own version of the conversation.

A reporter is interviewing Dr. Zee in the lab.
**Reporter:** We're here observing the famous Dr. Zee in <u>his chemistry</u> lab. What are you doing, Dr. Zee?
**Dr. Zee:** I'm doing an important experiment.
**Reporter:** What are you using, Dr. Zee?
**Dr. Zee:** I'm using <u>a Bunsen burner, a beaker of water</u>, and some <u>coffee</u>.
**Reporter:** Fascinating! Dr. Zee is putting <u>the beaker on the Bunsen burner</u>. Why are you doing that?
**Dr. Zee:** Because <u>I need hot water for my coffee</u>!

## Music (Dictionary, p. 120)

### *WOULD + RATHER* FOR PREFERENCE

*Which instrument would you rather hear, a piano or an accordion?*

**Interview**
Teacher's Notes, p. 10

Copy the questions (or the alternative questions) below on a copy of the Interview worksheet (p. 11). Follow the directions on the worksheet to have pairs write their own short answers and then their partners' short answers. Have students write follow-up sentences based on the interview answers.

**Interview Questions**
1. Which instrument would you rather hear right now, a piano or an accordion?
2. Which instrument would you rather hear right now, a tuba or a trumpet?
3. Which instrument would you rather hear right now, a flute or a clarinet?
4. Which instrument would you rather hear right now, a violin or a cello?

**Alternative Questions**
1. Which instrument would you rather play in a rock band, the drums or the guitar?
2. Which instrument would you rather play in an orchestra, the piano or the xylophone?
3. Which instrument would you rather learn to play, the tambourine or the bass?
4. Which would you rather do, sing in a band or play an instrument in a band?

## More School Subjects (Dictionary, p. 121)

### PRESENT PERFECT: *YES/NO* QUESTIONS

**Around the Table**
Teacher's Notes, p. 7

*Have you ever taken an art class? Yes, I have. Joe's taken an art class, and he's taken driver's education.*

Practice the question-and-answer forms as well as the affirmative and negative statements. Form groups of four students and assign roles A through D in each group. Have students conduct the drills.

***Yes/No* Questions**
Student A: Have you ever taken art?
Student B: Yes, I have. How about you? Have you ever taken art?
Student C: No, I haven't. How about you? Have you ever taken art?
Student D: Yes, I have. How about you? Have you ever taken art?
Student A answers and then asks the question again, substituting another class.

## North America and Central America (Dictionary, pp. 122–123)

### ADVERBS: *NORTH, SOUTH, EAST, WEST*

**Tic-Tac-Toe**
Teacher's Notes, p. 8

*Where's Ontario? It's in Canada, east of Manitoba.*

Copy the Tic-Tac-Toe grid onto the board or an overhead transparency. Play the game, using the suggested prompts.

| | | |
|---|---|---|
| Illinois | Puerto Rico | Ontario |
| Oregon | British Colombia | Wyoming |
| Costa Rica | Haiti | Vermont |

Prompt: *Where's...* ?
Students respond with *It's in* [state/region]... , based on the map in the dictionary.

## The World (Dictionary, pp. 124–125)

### *WH-* QUESTIONS: *WHERE*

**Board Race**
Teacher's Notes, p. 6

*Where's Bolivia? It's in South America. Where's Iceland? It's near Greenland.*

Ask the questions below. Have teams check the dictionary page and race to write the complete answers on the board.

| Questions | Answers |
|---|---|
| **1.** Where's Bolivia? | **1.** It's in South America. |
| **2.** Where's Iceland? | **2.** It's near Greenland. |
| **3.** Where's Cambodia? | **3.** It's in Asia. |
| **4.** Where's Zambia? | **4.** It's in Africa. |
| **5.** Where's The Sudan? | **5.** It's in Africa. |
| **6.** Where are the Hawaiian Islands? | **6.** They're in the North Pacific Ocean. |
| **7.** Where is Liechtenstein? | **7.** It's in Europe. |

## PRESENT PERFECT; COMPOUND SENTENCES WITH *AND, BUT*

**Answers Up**
Teacher's Notes, p. 2

*Jay has been to Ireland, but he hasn't been to Scotland.*

Make each statement below. Have students indicate which conjunction they heard by holding up the card labeled "BUT" or the card labeled "AND."

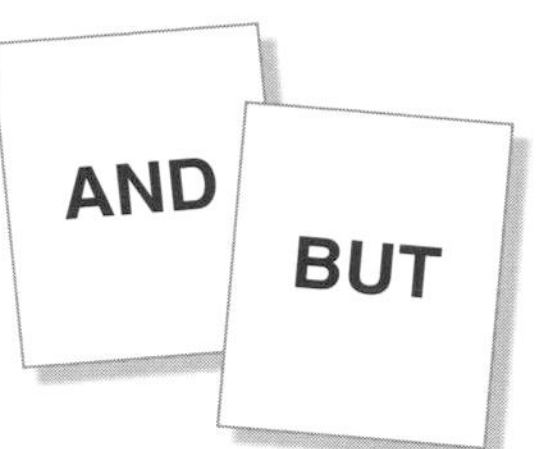
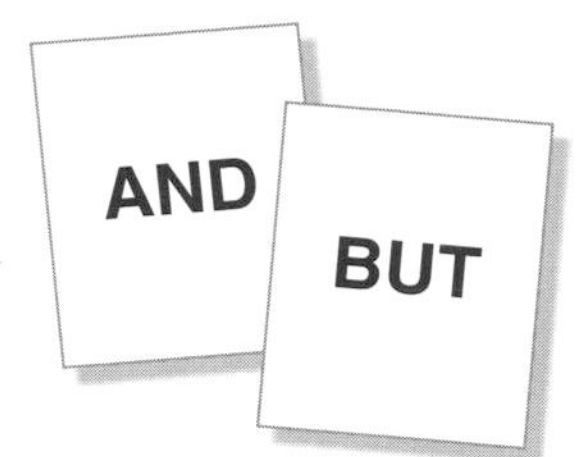


1. Jay has been to Ireland, but he hasn't been to Scotland.
2. Pat has been to Russia, and she's been to China.
3. Tom's been to South America, but he's never been to Bolivia.
4. Nan has been to South America, and she's been to Mexico.
5. Tim's been to Indonesia, and he's been to Vietnam.
6. Joe's never been to France, and he's never been to Germany.
7. Lara's been to Japan, but she hasn't been to Korea.
8. Rena's been to India, but she hasn't been to Pakistan.
9. Sam's never been to New Zealand, but he's been to Australia three times.
10. Tina's been to Sweden, she's been to Norway, and she's been to Finland.

# Energy and the Environment (Dictionary, p. 126)

## SIMPLE PRESENT: *WH-* QUESTIONS: *HOW, WHICH, WHEN, WHO, WHAT*

**Interview**
Teacher's Notes, p. 10

*How do you conserve energy? I turn off the lights.*

Copy the questions (or the alternative questions) below on a copy of the Interview worksheet (p. 11). Follow the directions on the worksheet to have pairs write their own short answers and then their partners' short answers. Have students write follow-up sentences based on the interview answers.

**Interview Questions**

1. How do you conserve energy?
2. How do you conserve water?
3. What kind of things do you recycle?
4. When do you use the most energy —in the summer or the winter?

**Alternative Questions**

1. Who uses the most energy in your home?
2. How do you fight pollution?
3. In your opinion, what type of pollution is the most dangerous?
4. In your opinion, which is the best energy resource?

# The Universe (Dictionary, p. 127)

## SIMPLE PRESENT; ORDINAL NUMBERS

**Peer Dictation**
Teacher's Notes, p. 3

*Mercury is the first planet from the sun.*

Write the sentences below on the board or on an overhead transparency, and conceal them from the class. Present the clarification strategy: *Which planet?* Pair students and assign A/B roles. (Have students sit so that the student who is dictating can see the sentences, but the one who is writing cannot.) Student A dictates first, and then Student B. Have partners check each other's work.

**A Sentences**

1. Mercury is the first planet from the sun.
2. Venus is the second planet from the sun.
3. Earth is the third planet from the sun.
4. Mars is the fourth planet from the sun.

**B Sentences**

1. Jupiter is the fifth planet from the sun.
2. Saturn is the sixth planet from the sun.
3. Uranus is the seventh planet from the sun.
4. Neptune is the eighth planet from the sun, and Pluto is the ninth.

## Trees and Plants (Dictionary, p. 128)

### SUPERLATIVES

*Redwood trees are the tallest trees in the world.*

**Mark My Words**
Teacher's Notes, p. 9

Write the sentences below on the board. Have students determine which sentences contain a mistake and which are correct. Then have teams take turns circling the errors and writing the correct sentences.

1. Redwood trees are the most tall trees in the world.
2. The wood from oak trees is one of the most strong woods you can buy.
3. Some of the prettiest flowers in the spring bloom on dogwood trees.
4. Pine trees are the popularest trees at Christmas time.
5. Poison oak is the dangerousest plant on the West Coast.
6. One of the most painful things you can do is sit on a cactus.

**Corrections: 1.** tallest; **2.** strongest; **3.** OK; **4.** most popular; **5.** most dangerous; **6.** OK

## Flowers (Dictionary, p. 129)

### SUPERLATIVES

*I want to buy the most beautiful flowers in the world.*

**Back and Forth**
Teacher's Notes, p. 14

Put the model conversation on the board. Introduce the situation and role-play the conversation with a volunteer. Have students form pairs and role-play their own version of the conversation.

A florist and a customer are discussing a gift.

**Florist:** Welcome to The Best Flower Shop. How may I help you?
**Customer:** I want to buy the most beautiful flowers in the world for my friend.
**Florist:** Tell me about your friend.
**Customer:** Well, she's the most wonderful person I know.
**Florist:** OK. These roses are the best flowers in the shop. They're only $100 a bunch.
**Customer:** Wait! I said the most beautiful, not the most expensive!
**Florist:** OK, here some nice carnations. They're the least expensive, but the most colorful!

## Marine Life, Amphibians, and Reptiles (Dictionary, pp. 130–131)

### COMPARATIVES; *WH-* QUESTIONS: *WHICH*

*Which is smaller—a tuna or a cod? A cod is smaller than a tuna.*

**Board Race**
Teacher's Notes, p. 6

Ask the questions below. Have teams check the dictionary page and race to write the complete answers on the board.

| Questions | Answers |
|---|---|
| **1.** Which is smaller—a tuna or a cod? | **1.** A cod is smaller than a tuna. |
| **2.** Which is larger—a sea urchin or a flounder? | **2.** A flounder is larger than a sea urchin. |
| **3.** Which is faster—a shark or a starfish? | **3.** A shark is faster than a starfish. |
| **4.** Which is smarter—a jellyfish or an octopus? | **4.** An octopus is smarter than a jellyfish. |
| **5.** Which is less dangerous—a crab or a worm? | **5.** A worm is less dangerous than a crab. |
| **6.** Which is more colorful—a mussel or a ray? | **6.** A ray is more colorful than a mussel. |

## Birds, Insects, and Arachnids (Dictionary, p. 132)

### POSSESSIVE NOUNS

*Penguins' wings do not have feathers. A spider's web is its dinner plate.*

**Peer Dictation**
Teacher's Notes, p. 3

Write the sentences below on the board or on an overhead transparency, and conceal them from the class. Present the clarification strategy: *Whose?* Pair students and assign A/B roles. (Have students sit so that the student who is dictating can see the sentences, but the one who is writing cannot.) Student A dictates first, and then Student B. Have partners check each other's work.

**A Sentences**

1. Penguins' wings do not have feathers.
2. Peacocks' tail feathers are colorful.
3. Hummingbirds' wings can move 70 times per second.
4. A woodpecker's beak is its fork.

**B Sentences**

1. A spider's web is its dinner plate.
2. A butterfly's wings are usually very colorful.
3. A ladybug's back is red with black spots.
4. A wasp's sting is its protection.

## Domestic Animals and Rodents (Dictionary, p. 133)

### ADJECTIVES AFTER *BE*

*Kitten are small.*

**Around the Table**
Teacher's Notes, p. 7

Practice the affirmative and negative statements as well as the question-and-answer forms. Form groups of four students and assign roles A through D in each group. Have students conduct the drills.

**Round 1: Affirmative Statements**
Student A: Kittens are small.
Student B: Rabbits are quiet.
Etc.

**Round 2: Negative Statements**
Student A: Puppies aren't quiet.
Student B: Cows aren't small.
Etc.

**Round 3: *Yes/No* Questions**
Student A: Are goldfish noisy?
Student B: No, they aren't. Are dogs friendly?
Student C: Yes, they are. Are pigs intelligent?
Etc.

## Mammals (Dictionary, pp. 134–135)

### ARTICLES: *A, THE,* AND NO ARTICLE

*The lion is a very powerful animal. Lions are meat eaters. I saw a lion…*

**Mark My Words**
Teacher's Notes, p. 9

Write the sentences below on the board. Have students determine which sentences contain a mistake and which are correct. Then have teams take turns circling the errors and writing the correct sentences.

1. The kangaroo has baby in its pouch.
2. Lion in the picture has a mane.
3. Pandas live in China.
4. The camel has hump.
5. He saw llama in Peru.
6. Gray wolf lives in North America.
7. The elephant has the long trunk.
8. I love the zebra's black and white stripes.

**Corrections: 1.** a baby; **2.** The lion; **3.** OK; **4.** a hump; **5.** a llama; **6.** The gray wolf; **7.** a long trunk; **8.** OK

## Jobs and Occupations, A–H (Dictionary, pp. 136–137)

### SIMPLE PRESENT: THIRD-PERSON SINGULAR AND PLURAL

**Answers Up**
Teacher's Notes, p. 2

*An architect designs buildings. Florists sell flowers.*

Make each statement below. Have students hold up the card labeled "VERB" to indicate that they heard the third-person plural form of the verb or the card labeled "VERB + *-S/-ES*" to indicate that they heard a third-person singular form.

1. An architect designs buildings.
2. Florists sell flowers.
3. Cashiers take money and make change.
4. Butchers cut meat.
5. A commercial fisher catches fish.
6. A garment worker makes clothes.
7. Carpenters build bookcases, furniture, and houses.
8. A doctor examines patients.
9. Engineers and architects usually work together.
10. Dentists check their patients' teeth.

## Jobs and Occupations, H–W (Dictionary, pp. 138–139)

### PREPOSITIONS WITH *WORK: FOR, WITH, ON*

**Peer Dictation**
Teacher's Notes, p. 3

*Interpreters often work for the government. Teachers work with students. Repair people work on broken machines.*

Write the sentences below on the board or on an overhead transparency, and conceal them from the class. Present the clarification strategies: *Who?* and *What do they do?* Pair students and assign A/B roles. (Have students sit so that the student who is dictating can see the sentences, but the one who is writing cannot.) Student A dictates first, and then Student B. Have partners check each other's work.

**A Sentences**
1. Interpreters often work for the government.
2. Repair people work on broken machines.
3. Teachers work with students.
4. Some writers work for magazines.

**B Sentences**
1. Sanitation workers often work for a city.
2. Veterinarians work with animals
3. Students work on homework.
4. Reporters often work for newspapers.

## Job Skills (Dictionary, p. 140)

### *CAN* FOR ABILITY; SUBJECT PRONOUNS

**Class Go-Around**
Teacher's Notes, p. 5

*She can type. He can supervise people. I can drive a truck.*

Have students look at the dictionary page as you identify all the different skills that you have. Start the chain drill by saying the first sentence below. Have a student repeat what you've said (changing the subject pronoun appropriately) and add his or her own skill. Continue the chain with at least five more students, each one repeating what has been said, changing the pronouns and adding another skill.

**T:** I can type.
**S1:** She can type, and I can supervise people.
**S2:** She can type, he can supervise people, and I can drive a truck.

## Job Search (Dictionary, p. 141)

### PRESENT CONTINUOUS VS. SIMPLE PRESENT

**TPR Grammar**
Teacher's Notes, p. 4

*What's she/he doing? What do you do when you want a job?*

Write three jobs on the board with a phone number beneath each job listing. Command individuals to perform the actions below. While students are performing each action, ask the class Question #1 to elicit present continuous statements. Then ask Question #2 to elicit simple present statements.

| Teacher Commands | Question #1 | Question #2 |
|---|---|---|
| Call for information. | What's she/he doing? | What do you say when you call for information? |
| Fill out a job application. | What's she/he doing? | What do you write on an application? |
| Go on an interview with [student's name]. | What's she/he doing? | What do you talk about on an interview? |
| Ask questions about the job. | What's she/he doing? | What do you ask about the job? |
| Thank the interviewer. | What's she/he doing? | What do you do after every interview? |

## An Office (Dictionary, pp. 142–143)

### *CAN* FOR ABILITY

**Interview**
Teacher's Notes, p. 10

*Can you type? Can you file?*

Copy the questions (or the alternative questions) below on a copy of the Interview worksheet (p. 11). Follow the directions on the worksheet to have pairs write their own short answers and then their partners' short answers. Have students write follow-up sentences based on the interview answers.

| Interview Questions | Alternative Questions |
|---|---|
| **1.** Can you type? | **1.** Can you use a fax machine? |
| **2.** Can you file? | **2.** Can you use a photocopier? |
| **3.** Can you transcribe notes? | **3.** Can you use a calculator? |
| **4.** Can you take messages? | **4.** Can you use a paper shredder? |

## Computers (Dictionary, p. 144)

### PREPOSITIONS OF PLACE: *IN, BEHIND, NEXT TO, IN FRONT OF, BETWEEN, ON THE RIGHT/LEFT*

**Board Race**
Teacher's Notes, p. 6

*It's between the mouse and the scanner.*

Ask the questions below. Have teams check the dictionary pages and race to write the complete answers on the board.

| Where's.... | Answers |
|---|---|
| **1.** the CD-ROM? | **1.** It's in the disc drive. |
| **2.** the mouse? | **2.** It's in front of the keyboard. |
| **3.** the joystick? | **3.** It's between the mouse and the scanner. |
| **4.** the modem? | **4.** It's next to the monitor, on the right. |
| **5.** the CPU? | **5.** It's next to the monitor, on the left. |
| **6.** the scanner? | **6.** It's in front of the printer, on the right. |
| **7.** the keyboard? | **7.** It's between the mouse and monitor. |
| **8.** the printer? | **8.** It's behind the surge protector. |

## A Hotel (Dictionary, p. 145)

### *WH-* QUESTIONS: *WHO, WHERE*

**Answers Up**
Teacher's Notes, p. 2

*Who is in the lobby? Where is the doorman?*

Make each statement below. Leave out the key words by saying "blah blah." Have students indicate which clarification question to ask by holding up the card labeled "WHO?" or the card labeled "WHERE?"

1. The "blah, blah" is in the lobby, near the door.
2. The doorman is in front of the "blah, blah."
3. The desk clerk is behind the "blah, blah."
4. The housekeeper is in the "blah, blah," making the bed.
5. Room service is in the "blah, blah."
6. The "blah, blah" is getting ice at the ice machine.
7. The "blah, blah" is buying a gift.
8. Two servers are setting the table in the "blah, blah."

## A Factory (Dictionary, p. 146)

### SIMPLE PRESENT; ADVERBS OF SEQUENCE

**Peer Dictation**
Teacher's Notes, p. 3

*First the factory owner has an idea. Next the designer designs the product.*

Write the sentences below on the board or on an overhead transparency, and conceal them from the class. Present the clarification strategy: *One more time?* Pair students and assign A/B roles. (Have students sit so that the student who is dictating can see the sentences, but the one who is writing cannot.) Student A dictates first, and then Student B. Have partners check each other's work.

**A Sentences**
1. First the factory owner has an idea for a new product.
2. Next the designer designs the product.
3. Then the factory manufactures the product.
4. Finally the factory ships the products.

**B Sentences**
1. First the workers assemble the product.
2. Next the packers put the products into boxes.
3. After that the customers order the product.
4. Then the order pullers pull the orders from the warehouse.

## Job Safety (Dictionary, p. 147)

### *MUST* AND *MUST NOT*

**Sentence Maker**
Teacher's Notes, p. 12

*Construction workers must wear hard hats. Cafeteria workers must not be careless.*

Write the words below on a copy of the Sentence Maker grid (p. 13). Duplicate and cut apart one set of word cards for each group of four to six students.* Have each group use their cards to make sentences, while a group recorder writes them on a separate sheet of paper. Instruct students to make and record as many sentences as they can.

| | | | | | |
|---|---|---|---|---|---|
| Construction | Cafeteria | Factory | workers | must | not |
| be | careless | careful | smoke | forget | to |
| wear | safety glasses | hard hats | earplugs | latex gloves | hair nets |

*__Note:__ Students will not use the question mark for this activity. Questions with *must* are not common in American English.

## Farming and Ranching (Dictionary, p. 148)

### SIMPLE PRESENT VS. PRESENT CONTINUOUS

**Mark My Words**
Teacher's Notes, p. 9

*The hired hand usually feeds the cattle at 7:00 a.m. He's planting alfalfa right now.*

Write the sentences below on the board. Have students determine which sentences contain a mistake and which are correct. Then have teams take turns circling the errors and writing the correct sentences.

1. The hired hand usually is feeding the cattle at 7:00 a.m.
2. He plants alfalfa right now.
3. The farmworkers harvest the corn every year.
4. The farmer driving the tractor to the vineyard every afternoon.
5. The horses usually eating hay.
6. The rancher is fixing his fence.
7. At this moment, the farmer milk the cows.

**Corrections: 1.** feeds; **2.** is planting; **3.** OK; **4.** drives; **5.** eat; **6.** OK; **7.** is milking

## Construction (Dictionary, p. 149)

### *CAN* FOR ABILITY AND POSSIBILITY

**Around the Table**
Teacher's Notes, p. 7

*Can you operate a cherry picker? What can you do with a hammer?*

Practice the question-and-answer forms. Form groups of four students and assign roles A through D in each group. Have students conduct the Q&A drills.

**Round 1: *Yes/No* Questions (Ability)**
Student A: Can you operate a jackhammer?
Student B: No, I can't, but I'd like to learn how. Can you operate a cherry picker?
Student C: Yes, I can. Can you operate a bulldozer?
Etc.

**Round 2: *Yes/No* Questions (Possibility)**
Student A: What can you do with a hammer?
Student B: You can hammer a nail. What can you do with a trowel?
Etc.

## Tools and Building Supplies (Dictionary, pp. 150–151)

### PREPOSITIONS OF PLACE: *ON, IN, ON THE RIGHT/LEFT*

**Back and Forth**
Teacher's Notes, p. 14

*Where are the nails? They're on the hardware aisle, on the right side.*

Put the model conversation on the board. Introduce the situation and role-play the conversation with a volunteer. Have students form pairs and role-play their own version of the conversation.

A customer is talking to a clerk in a building supply store.
**Customer:** Excuse me. Where can I find the nails?
**Clerk:** The nails are on the hardware aisle, on the right side.
**Customer:** Are they toward the front or the back?
**Clerk:** They're toward the front.
**Customer:** Thanks. Oh! Where can I find a circular saw?
**Clerk:** All our circular saws are in the power tools section.
**Customer:** Let's see. That's nails on the hardware aisle, circular saws in the power tools section. Thanks!

## Places to Go (Dictionary, p. 152)

**SIMPLE PAST: *BE;* PREPOSITIONS OF PLACE: *AT***

**Class Go-Around**
Teacher's Notes, p. 5

*Where were you yesterday? I was at the zoo.*

Have students look at the dictionary page as you identify where you were yesterday. Start the chain drill by saying the first sentence below. Have a student repeat what you've said (changing the subject pronoun appropriately) and add a statement about his or her own location. Continue the chain with at least five more students, each one repeating what has been said and adding his or her own location.

**T:** I was at the zoo.
**S1:** She was at the zoo, and I was at the art museum.
**S2:** She was at the zoo, he was at the art museum, and I was at the swap meet.

## The Park and Playground (Dictionary, p. 153)

**FUTURE: *WILL***

**Sentence Maker**
Teacher's Notes, p. 12

*We'll picnic in the park next Saturday. Next week they won't go to the park.*

Write the words below on a copy of the Sentence Maker grid (p. 13). Duplicate and cut apart one set of word cards for each group of four to six students. Have each group use their cards to make sentences or questions, while a group recorder writes them on a separate sheet of paper. Instruct students to make and record as many sentences or questions as they can.

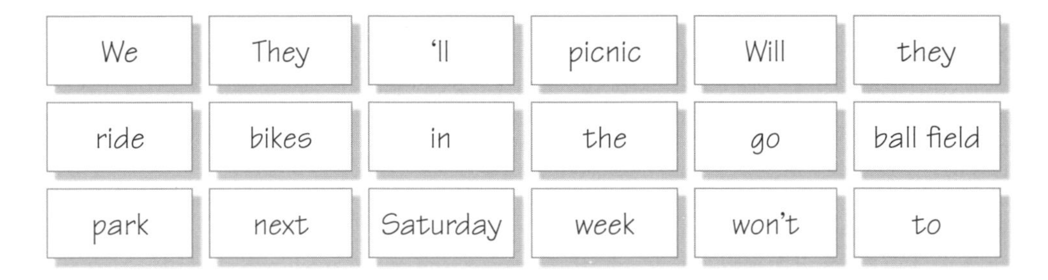


## Outdoor Recreation, The Beach (Dictionary, pp. 154, 155)

**FUTURE: *GOING TO***

**Peer Dictation**
Teacher's Notes, p. 3

*Thomas is going to go mountain biking. They're going to walk on the pier.*

Write the sentences below on the board or an overhead transparency, and conceal them from the class. Present the clarification strategy: *Going to what?* Pair students and assign A/B roles. (Have students sit so that the student who is dictating can see the sentences, but the one who is writing cannot.) Student A dictates first, and then Student B. Have partners check each other's work.

**A Sentences**

1. Thomas and Martha are going to go camping on their vacation.
2. Martha isn't going to go backpacking.
3. She's going to go horseback riding.
4. Thomas is going to go mountain biking.

**B Sentences**

1. Maureen and Mo are going to go to the beach on their vacation.
2. They're not going to swim in the ocean.
3. They're going to sit under their beach umbrella and read.
4. They're also going to walk on the pier.

## Sports Verbs (Dictionary, pp. 156–157)

### FUTURE: *GOING TO*

**TPR Grammar**
Teacher's Notes, p. 4

*He's going to walk to the door. She's going to run to the back of the room.*

Command individuals and groups to perform the actions below. Before students perform each action, ask the class the questions to elicit future statements.

| **Teacher Commands** | **Teacher Questions** |
|---|---|
| Walk to the door. | What are they going to do? |
| Run to the back of the room. | What's she going to do? |
| Catch this eraser. | What's he going to do? |
| Jump three times. | What are they going to do? |
| Race me to the desk. | What's he going to do? |
| Throw your eraser to me. | What's she going to do? |
| Jog around your desk. | What are you going to do? |

## Team Sports, Individual Sports (Dictionary, pp. 158–159)

### COMPOUND SENTENCES WITH *BUT, AND;* ADVERBS OF ADDITION: *TOO*

**Around the Table**
Teacher's Notes, p. 7

*I don't like archery, but I love bowling. You like softball, and I like it too.*

Practice statements with *but* and *and.* Form groups of four students and assign roles A through D in each group. Have students conduct the drills.

**Round 1: Statements *(but)***
Student A: I don't like archery, but I love fencing.
Student B: I don't like volleyball, but I love basketball.
Student C: I don't like inline skating, but I love skateboarding.
Student D: I don't like baseball, but I love soccer.

**Round 2: Statements *(and)***
Student A: You like pool, and I like it too.
Student B: You like softball, and I like it too.
Student C: You like wrestling, and I like it too.
Student D: You like ice hockey, and I like it too.

## Winter Sports and Water Sports (Dictionary, p. 160)

### GERUNDS AFTER *GO*

**Sentence Maker**
Teacher's Notes, p. 12

*He goes ice skating every winter. Does he go surfing every summer?*

Write the words below on a copy of the Sentence Maker grid (p. 13). Duplicate and cut apart one set of word cards for each group of four to six students. Have each group use their cards to make sentences or questions, while a group recorder writes them on a separate sheet of paper. Instruct students to make and record as many sentences or questions as they can.

| | | | | | |
|---|---|---|---|---|---|
| Does | he | go | ice skating | every | winter |
| He | goes | surfing | summer | she | sailing |
| skiing | She | doesn't | does | When | Where |

## Sports Equipment (Dictionary, p. 161)

### SIMPLE PRESENT: AFFIRMATIVE AND NEGATIVE STATEMENTS

**Answers Up**
Teacher's Notes, p. 2

*This store carries archery equipment. It doesn't carry any fencing equipment.*

Make each statement below. Have students indicate whether they heard the affirmative or the negative form of the verb *(not, n't)* by holding up the card labeled "+" (for affirmative) or "–" (for negative).

1. There are several flying discs for sale at this store.
2. There aren't many bowling balls for sale.
3. The salesman isn't holding a pair of inline skates.
4. He has one skate in his left hand and a hockey stick in his right hand.
5. The customer is holding a pair of weights.
6. He isn't going to buy them because they aren't heavy enough.
7. This store carries archery equipment.
8. It doesn't carry any fencing equipment.
9. There aren't many customers in the store.
10. There's only one customer, and he's leaving.

## Hobbies and Games (Dictionary, pp. 162–163)

### SIMPLE PRESENT: QUESTIONS; ADVERBS OF FREQUENCY

**Interview**
Teacher's Notes, p. 10

*How often do you play chess? Do you play cards? What other games do you play?*

Copy the questions (or the alternative questions) below on a copy of the Interview worksheet (p. 11). Follow the directions on the worksheet to have pairs write their own short answers and then their partners' short answers. Have students write follow-up sentences based on the interview answers.

**Interview Questions**
1. How often do you play chess?
2. Do you play cards?
3. What other games do you play?
4. How often do you knit?

**Alternative Questions**
1. Do you build models?
2. What other crafts do you do?
3. How often do you paint?
4. Did you pretend when you were a child?

## Electronics and Photography (Dictionary, pp. 164–165)

### *WOULD* FOR POLITENESS

**Back and Forth**
Teacher's Notes, p. 14

*I'd like to return this cassette recorder. Would you like a new cassette recorder?*

Put the model conversation on the board. Introduce the situation and role-play the conversation with volunteers. Have students form groups of three and role-play their own version of the conversation.

A customer wants to return a purchase.
**Customer:** Hello. I'd like to return <u>this cassette recorder</u>.
**Clerk:** What's the matter with <u>it</u>?
**Customer:** When I opened the box, <u>it was broken</u>.
**Manager:** Is there a problem?
**Clerk:** <u>She</u>'d like to return <u>this cassette recorder</u>. <u>It doesn't work</u>.
**Manager:** OK. Would you like <u>a new cassette recorder</u>?
**Customer:** No, I'd like to get my money back.
**Manager:** Certainly. Come with me.

## Entertainment (Dictionary, pp. 166–167)

### SIMPLE PAST VS. SIMPLE PRESENT

**Interview**
Teacher's Notes, p. 10

*What was the last movie you saw? What kind of movies do you like?*

Copy the questions (or the alternative questions) below on a copy of the Interview worksheet (p. 11). Follow the directions on the worksheet to have pairs write their own short answers and then their partners' short answers. Have students write follow-up sentences based on the interview answers.

**Interview Questions**
1. What was the last movie you saw?
2. What kind of movies do you like?
3. Did you watch TV yesterday?
4. What TV programs do you watch?

**Alternative Questions**
1. What kind of books do you read?
2. What was the last book you read?
3. Did you go to any concerts last year?
4. What radio programs do you listen to?

## Holidays (Dictionary, p. 168)

### *WH-* QUESTIONS: *WHO, WHAT, WHERE, WHEN*

**Mark My Words**
Teacher's Notes, p. 9

*When is New Year's Day?*

Write the sentences below on the board. Have students determine which sentences contain a mistake and which are correct. Then have teams take turns circling the errors and writing the correct sentences.

1. When does New Year's Day?
2. What do people do on New Year's Day?
3. Where you do go on the Fourth of July?
4. What is the date for next Thanksgiving?
5. What do you eating on Thanksgiving?
6. Where do Valentine's Day—February 14 or March 14?
7. What is children does on Halloween?

**Corrections: 1.** is ; **2.** OK; **3.** do you go; **4.** OK; **5.** eat; **6.** When is; **7.** do children do

## A Party (Dictionary, p. 169)

### FUTURE, PRESENT CONTINUOUS AND SIMPLE PAST

**TPR Grammar**
Teacher's Notes, p. 4

*He'll hide. He's hiding. He hid*

Command individuals and groups to perform the actions below. Before students perform an action, ask the class Question #1 to elicit a future statement. Then, while students are performing the action, ask the class Question #2 to elicit a present continuous statement. Finally, after students perform the action, ask the class Question #3 to elicit a simple past statement.

| Command | Question #1 | Question #2 | Question #3 |
|---|---|---|---|
| Decorate the classroom. | What will they do? | What are they doing? | What did they do? |
| Wrap this gift. | What will he do? | What is he doing? | What did he do? |
| Hide and wait. | What will he do? | What is he doing? | What did he do? |
| Open the door. | What will she do? | What is she doing? | What did she do? |
| Shout "Surprise!" | What will you do? | What are you doing? | What did you do? |
| Sing "Happy Birthday." | What will you do? | What are you doing? | What did you do? |
| Open your presents. | What will she do? | What is she doing? | What did she do? |
| Thank everyone. | What will she do? | What is she doing? | What did she do? |

# Grammar Index